The Gifted Kids Survival Guide II

The Gifted Kids Survival Guide II

A Sequel to the Original
Gifted Kids Survival Guide (For Ages 11–18)

James R. Delisle and Judy Galbraith

Edited by Pamela Espeland

Illustrated by Harry Pulver Jr.

Free Spirit PUBLISHING

Library of Congress Cataloging-in-Publication Data

Delisle, James R.
   The gifted kids survival guide II.

   Sequel to: The gifted kids survival guide / Judy Galbraith.
   For GTs ages 11–18.
   Includes index.
   Summary: Examines the problems of gifted and talented teenagers and explains how they can make the best use of their educational opportunities, get along better with parents and friends, and understand themselves better. Includes a section in which gifted individuals speak out.

   1. Gifted children—Juvenile literature.
2. Gifted children—Education—Juvenile literature.
[1. Gifted children] I. Galbraith, Judy. II. Pulver, Harry, ill. III. Galbraith, Judy. Gifted kids survival guide. IV. Title.
HQ773.5.D44   1987   371.95   87-80584
ISBN 0-915793-09-1 (pbk.)

10 9 8 7 6 5 4 3

Printed in the United States of America

Cover and book design by Nancy MacLean
and Mike Tuminelly

Free Spirit Publishing Co.
123 N. Third St., Suite 716
Minneapolis, MN 55401

DEDICATION

To Leo and Marie, Wilson and Marion,
Tom and Cheryl, Deb and Matt:

They are parents
. . . and they are family
. . . and they are loved.

A special thank you to Mr. Maloney, who instilled in me the courage to encounter, discuss, and act upon topics that "aren't gonna go away" just because they're ignored.

J.D.

Many heartfelt thanks to . . .
. . . the young people who generously offered their insights, experiences, and ideas during the writing of this book, and to
. . . Ann Stefanson for teaching me about honesty, and for helping me to be kind to myself.

Judy G.

CONTENTS

INTRODUCTION

The Gifted Kids Survival Guide II is a sequel to the original *Gifted Kids Survival Guide*, first published in 1983. It isn't mean to replace the previous *GKSG* but to follow it — to continue the work begun by its predecessor.

▶ Why a sequel?

When readers commented on the original *GKSG*, they said that they wished there had been more information about giftedness, IQ (what it does and doesn't mean), testing, and intelligence. They wanted more ideas about making school better for them, handling the expectations of others, and making and keeping friends.

Judy received tons of letters from kids who wanted to know what else she was writing. Jim received quite a few, too, from kids all over who are curious and concerned about growing up gifted. Many wrote to say, "I'm so relieved to know that I'm not the only one who thinks about these things!"

▶ Why a collaboration — why TWO authors?

We believe that any type of educational research is good only if kids (the students who are the recipients of our research results) say, "I believe that. It makes a lot of sense to me. It's relevant to my life."

Both of us have spent a great deal of time working with and interviewing gifted and talented students (GTs). We ask them what they feel, what they think, and what we can do to help. We think that sharing our findings and experiences makes for a better book and one that's more useful to you.

We've been very concerned with the school issues GTs face; many are "learning to underachieve." Many have basic questions like "How am I the same as other gifted kids? How am I different?"

1

Sometimes the points GTs make don't solve any problems. But if you know that somebody 2,000 miles away (or just across town) is thinking the same things you are, that, in itself, can be therapeutic. It's reassuring when someone else says what you're thinking. It's easier than saying it yourself and risking being thought of as "weird."

We want this book to put you in touch with other kids who think and feel as you do. We also want to provide you with some strategies for getting more out of schools, making friends, understanding who you are, and figuring out how to get what **you** want out of life.

▶ Who should read this book?

Although *GKSG II* has been written for GTs ages 11–18, we hope that some people under 11 will read it — and a lot of people over 18, including teachers and parents of GTs. We think it can give teachers and parents a clearer understanding of the GTs in their classrooms and their families.

Both of us have noticed that when a problem exists between teachers and/or parents and kids, it's often rooted in a lack of mutual respect. Parents or teachers may think, "You don't know anything because you're just a kid." Kids may think, "My teachers don't care about me because I'm one in a hundred" or "My parents figure that just because I'm gifted I should be able to do everything on my own." Each side is guilty of assuming that the other has little or nothing to offer.

On the other hand, we've noticed that problems between teachers and/or parents and kids seem to diminish when they learn to respect one another. We hope that this book will help teachers and parents become more respectful of the knowledge kids (especially bright kids) have. We want them to start asking, "What can I learn from *you?*"

We also hope that this book will help kids become more respectful of the wisdom and experience their teachers and parents bring to the relationship. That gets easier when the two sides stop arguing and working against each other. To that end, we have included several suggestions kids can use to get their needs met *constructively*, working *with* their parents and teachers whenever possible.

▶ How should I use this book?

Read it cover to cover, bit by bit, front to back, or back to front. Read it upside down, if you prefer. It's **your** book — use it as you like.

Some of the sections in it may be helpful immediately; others may not. Our research has shown that all of these topics are of interest to most gifted students at some time or another in their lives.

The section on teenage suicide and depression looks at a sensitive topic. We realize that relatively few people deal with these issues in their daily lives. Still, we think it's important to communicate the facts and the feelings associated with them. We *all* need to acknowledge that some people hurt bad; we *all* need to do what we can to help.

▶ What should I do after I read this book?

Take a nap, take a walk, take a trip around the world, or do nothing at all — then *write to us*. Tell us if and how this book affected you. Was it helpful? useful? interesting? boring? fun? deadly? just okay? What did you like about it? What didn't you like about it? What did we include that was especially important to you? What did we miss that you needed to know?

Often we're asked to speak to parent and teacher groups; if we know that this book made sense, or we could or should have said more (or less) about something, we can pass that message on to the adults in our audiences.

Write to us care of Free Spirit Publishing, 123 North Third Street, Suite 716, Minneapolis, MN 55401. We want to hear from you.

Meanwhile: Our best wishes to you for a happy, challenging life.

Jim Delisle and Judy Galbraith

INTELLIGENCE: TESTS DON'T TELL IT ALL

Several years ago, all schoolchildren in England were required to take tests at the end of the 5th grade. These tests were called the "11-plus exams," and they were used to determine who would eventually go to college — and who wouldn't.

Has a test ever been used to determine *your* future? Like whether you would get into a certain class . . . or maybe skip a grade . . . or make it into your school's GT program?

In England, the 11-plus exams were a Very Big Deal. If you did well, you were placed on the "honors track." If you did so-so, you were put into classes where not much was expected of you because (supposedly) you were "only average." And if you did uh-oh — if you bottomed out on the 11-plus — you went to a trade school. *Because you couldn't get in anywhere else.*

Sounds fair, right? Only if you agree that tests tell it all. But what if they don't?

Consider the cases of Jonathan, Helen, and Reginald (called Reggie by his friends).

- Jonathan had always been an above-average student. But during the time of the 11-plus exams, he was under the weather. Sick, in fact, with a cold that made him feel as if he was hearing and seeing the world through a mattress. His concerned mum gave him antihistamines. The result: Jonathan couldn't think straight. All the questions seemed to run together on the page. His mouth felt dry and his head buzzed. He did poorly on the exams.

   Jonathan's destiny? Trade School.

- Helen was an extremely creative student. Her short stories won prizes, and she played the oboe beautifully. Unfortunately, Helen was not a teacher-pleaser. Rather than answer the questions on the exam, she decided to form a pattern of interconnected dots on her answer sheet. The results were graphically interesting but less than satisfactory scorewise.

   Helen's fate? The Only Average School — with the recommendation that she become a nanny.

- Reggie had been a winner from way back. His mother had read to him when he was still in the womb, and by the time Reggie was 3 years old, he was reading books on his own (ones *without* pictures). Naturally, he practiced for the 11-plus exams. He was the first in his class to finish, and he got the highest score.

   Reggie's future? Anywhere he wanted to go — as long as he chose college. And anything he wanted to be — as long as he decided to become a professional.

What conclusions can we draw from these cases? Let's start with the obvious ones: Neither Jonathan nor Helen got what they deserved. Now let's look at the less obvious one: The same was true for Reggie.

Jonathan and Helen were told that they *couldn't* succeed. Reggie was told that he *had to* succeed. Jonathan and Helen were denied opportunities; Reggie was forced to take them, whether he wanted them or not.

Luckily for England, the 11-plus exams went the way of many bad ideas: down the tubes. Someone finally figured out that the only kids gaining access to the honors track were those who already had certain advantages, like wealthy parents and social standing. The exams were giving rise to an upper-class elite. Also, the trade school teachers resented being thought of as the dregs of the educational system. They knew that they (and their students) had talents, too, in mechanical, technical, or artistic areas.

U.S. educator and writer John Gardner put it this way:

> "The society which scorns excellence in plumbing because it is a humble activity and tolerates shoddiness in philosophy because it is an exalted activity will have neither good plumbing nor good philosophy. Neither its pipes nor its theories will hold water."

Western cultures have traditionally had a hard time understanding and identifying intelligence. For years, psychologists and educators have labored under the misconception that intellect can be measured with an hour-and-a-half test of verbal ability — like an IQ test. Only recently have people started realizing that there are lots of ways to be smart.

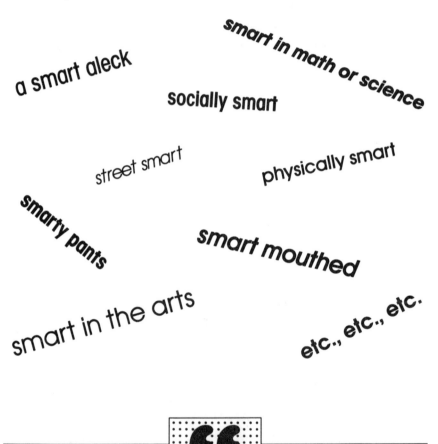

a smart aleck

smart in math or science

socially smart

street smart

physically smart

smarty pants

smart mouthed

smart in the arts

etc., etc., etc.

INTELLIGENCE THROUGH THE AGES: BLESSING OR CURSE?

People with high intelligence have been objects of curiosity and study throughout recorded history.

▶ More than 2,000 years ago, the Chinese instituted large-scale testing to determine which of their young people would make the best leaders.

▶ Around 1373 A.D., the Ottoman Turks identified young men with superior physical appearance and endurance.

▶ During the 1800s, Italian physician and criminologist Cesare Lombroso offered "scientific proof" that highly able individuals were freaks of nature and prone to insanity. French psychologist Alfred Binet (who, with Theodore Simon, developed one of the first intelligence tests) toyed with the notion that only a thin line separated genius from madness.

▶ Also during the 1800s, Sir Francis Galton decided that intelligence was 100 percent inherited, and that those who didn't measure up "could find welcome and a refuge in celibate monasteries or sisterhoods."

With all this historical baggage littering the field of intelligence, it's no surprise that our present-day culture still maintains a love/hate relationship with gifted persons. Four thousand plus years of thinking have resulted in such weird and contradictory conclusions as "giftedness = good looks" to "giftedness = craziness." Only within the past 50 years — a smidgen compared to the span of time humans have been upright bipeds — have people begun to examine intelligence on its own terms.

"Much learning does not teach a man to have intelligence."
— *Heraclitus*

It was a voice in the wilderness (actually, southern Indiana) that first hinted that giftedness was okay. In 1921, Lewis M. Terman started a study that continues today through the work of his research descendants. Terman examined the lives of 1,528 children with IQs of 140+. Simple arithmetic reveals that a child who was 12 in 1921 is now pushing the outer limits of Social Security, yet these same people and their progeny are still being analyzed by Terman's successors at Stanford University.

Here are a few of their findings:

▶ The exceptionally able students who were kept within their age groups instead of being placed with intellectual peers tended to develop lazy work habits.

▶ The most important companions to success were supportive parents, a built-in desire to excel, and self-confidence about one's ability to succeed.

▶ No one developed postadolescent stupidity. This finding helped erase the commonly held belief in "early ripe, early rot" — the conviction that gifted children get less intelligent with age.

Thanks in large part to Terman and his colleagues, giftedness began to be perceived as a positive attribute. Personal success and career satisfaction were associated with stability, not instability; with the absence, not the presence, of internal conflict; and with the support of others who also have above-average abilities — "in short," said Terman, "with well-balanced temperament and with freedom from excessive frustration."

Enter the Critics . . .

Given enough time and publicity, even the best research is found to be flawed. In the 1970s and right up to the present, Terman's research has been shown to be lacking in some areas. Not necessarily *wrong*, just *incomplete*.

While Terman helped disprove many of the negative stereotypes about giftedness, some people feel that he waxed too positive about it. Being gifted isn't all happiness and sunshine, as Terman seemed to imply. Also, several folks contested Terman's idea that giftedness = high IQ, arguing that intelligence is too complex to be measured by a one-shot test.

. . . And the (Research) Beat Goes On

Harvard researcher Howard Gardner believes that there are many forms of intelligence that aren't measured by typical paper-and-pencil tests. In his book, *Frames of Mind: The Theory of Multiple Intelligences*, he describes several forms of intelligence:

- linguistic intelligence
- musical intelligence
- spatial intelligence
- logical-mathematical intelligence
- bodily-kinesthetic intelligence
- personal intelligence

According to Gardner, it's possible to be gifted in one area and average or below- average in others. **But no intelligence is necessarily better — or worse — than any other.** This means that a person who can take apart and reassemble a Volkswagen without the help of an owner's manual is just as gifted as a person who takes the championship in a chess match. Both are gifted, but in different ways.

David Huang is a good example of Gardner's theory personified. As a college sophomore, David had a 3.7 grade point average. A typical semester course load for him included organic chemistry, biology, calculus, and microcomputer graphics. He planned to become a surgeon. His hobbies were bicycling and watching cartoons on TV — especially He-Man, Scooby-Doo, and Woody Woodpecker.

Watching cartoons? Isn't that a bit strange for a premed college student? Not if you consider one more important fact about David — his age. While most sophomores are 18 or 19, David was only 9 years old.

David possesses a high degree of logical-mathematical intelligence. But at age 9, he was still a kid who probably snacked on Twinkies and milk and had to be reminded to tie his shoelaces.

The beauty of Gardner's theory lies in the fact that you don't have to be #1 in everything in order to be considered gifted. You can have abilities in certain areas and still be a regular person.

"The test of a first-rate intelligence is the ability to hold two opposed ideas in the mind at the same time, and still retain the ability to function."
— *F. Scott Fitzgerald*

Another researcher, Yale psychology professor Robert Sternberg, is also a proponent of multiple intelligences. In his book, *Beyond IQ: A Triarchic Theory of Human Intelligence*, he contends that knowledge is only one part of intellect. It's not enough to *know* something, he says; you also need to be able to figure out how to solve problems.

Say, for example, that you're reading a book and come across the word *clandestine*. You've never seen it before in your life and have no idea what it means. Can you figure it out from the context — the words and concepts that surround it? If so, you're using a different form of intelligence than is generally measured on IQ tests.

Or you arrive home from your date two hours past curfew. You forgot to call your folks to tell them you'd be late (time flies when you're having fun!). You know you're in trouble, but instead of panicking, you try to read the situation by listening to your parents' complaints. Then, based on what they say, you take the direct approach:

To Dad: "Gee, Dad, I'm sorry. I bet *you* never put your folks through this much grief."
Dad's reaction *(although he might not say it)*: "Boys will be boys."

To Mom: "I should have called, and I'm sorry. Being forgetful is no excuse."
Mom's reaction *(although she might not say it)*: "She knows she was wrong and has learned her lesson, so I guess I don't have to punish her."

Nobody argues, everybody stays calm, and you all go to bed with smiles on your faces.

Maybe your parents will come back to you the next morning and say, "That was a pretty sneaky way to get out of being grounded." If this happens, you can respond, "Hey, I was just using my highly developed metaprocessing skills in the area of social relationships!" That's what Sternberg would say, and it sounds pretty good, doesn't it?

Sometimes, it pays to be smart.

"Intelligence is quickness to apprehend as distinct from ability, which is capacity to act wisely on the thing apprehended."
— *Alfred North Whitehead*

THE SCOOP ON
IQ TESTS

You probably already know that IQ stands for Intelligence Quotient. *Quotient* as in long division, because a person's IQ is determined by a simple mathematical formula:

$$\frac{\text{Mental Age}}{\text{Life Age}} \times 100 = \text{IQ}$$

Let's say that your life age (the number of years you've been on the planet) is 13. You take an IQ test — for example, the Stanford-Binet. The examiner computes your score by comparing your answers to those given by thousands of other people of various ages. If your responses are both accurate and sophisticated (that is, if you used logic or elaborated on your answers), chances are your thinking will be revealed as more like that of a 16-year-old than the 13-year-old you are. Thus, your *mental age* will be higher than your *life age*. And here's what will happen to the formula:

$$\frac{16 \text{ (mental age)}}{13 \text{ (life age)}} \times 100 = 123 \text{ IQ, 13 life age}$$

Since the average IQ is 100, an IQ of 123 would put you above average. Translated into percentiles, a 123 IQ ranks you at about the 92nd percentile, meaning that you scored higher than 92 out of 100 13-year-olds who took the same test.

There are other ways to compute IQ. For example, if you take the *Wechsler Intelligence Scale for Children — Revised*, your answers are compared to those given by other people the same life age as you. If your replies are superior to those of your chronological peers, you are considered "positively deviant" with an IQ of 120 or above. (If the phrase "positively deviant" reminds you of the old days when smart meant crazy, don't despair. In this case, the word *deviant* means "different from the norm.")

However IQ is measured, though, anything over 100 is above average. Some people cite 140 as the cutoff between smart and genius. Very generally speaking, an IQ around 130 indicates the presence of some solid intellectual muscle.

Of course, just because it's there doesn't mean it's being exercised.

And what if an obviously smart person ends up with a lower score? Should he or she give up, drop out, throw in the towel, and plan a future of daytime TV watching? What do *you* think?

There are those who say — and we agree — that **I Can** may be more important than **IQ**.

- -

SIX MORE POSSIBLE MEANINGS FOR THE ACRONYM IQ

Although IQ generally stands for Intelligence Quotient, you may be one of those rebellious types who think it could mean something else. Like any or all of the following:

I Quit

Some people believe that an average IQ dooms them to a life of menial jobs and low-quality relationships. Not so! IQ is only *one* way to measure intelligence, and it's by no means the last word. No one should be sentenced to a future of failure on the basis of a test score.

Inane Questions

When you look closely at some IQ tests, you can't help wondering if the people who concocted the questions are really yahoos disguised as experts. Who wants to be judged on the basis of whether he or she can define *uxoricide*? GET SERIOUS! (If you want to know, *uxoricide* is "the murder of one's wife.")

Individual Quirks

In one test you are asked to find the "best, most sensible" word to complete this sentence: "The foundation of all science is _____ ." From among these words — observation, invention, knowledge, theory, art — which do you feel fits? The test developers have one word in mind. But if your opinion differs, too bad. It's marked wrong. Hmmm.

Insufficient Quantity

Some IQ tests last only 20 minutes, which doesn't leave much time for revealing your specific strengths and weaknesses. If you're going to be placed in (or kept out of) a gifted program on the basis of your IQ, you deserve more than a third of an hour to show your stuff.

Intense Queasiness

Tests have been known to make people anxious. The typical IQ test is administered in a situation that is stressful and constrained by time limits. "Brain drain" isn't uncommon. You may forget everything you've learned in your entire life — only to recall it all five minutes after the test ends.

Impressive Quality

Although IQ tests are criticized, the fact remains that people with high IQs often do very well in life. The tests seem to do a good job of locating overall intelligence (a score of 150 usually isn't an accident). But do they skip over some very able people who just don't perform well on tests? The evidence points to **yes**.

The Hidden Dangers

James J. Gallagher, one of the best-known authors in the field of gifted education, has this to say about IQ:

> "In an era when our lives seem to be controlled and regulated by numbers — social security, telephone or credit card — a special place has been reserved for the IQ score. It has been said that once a person has received information about his or her IQ score, that number becomes indelibly etched in his cortex as if it had been burned there with hydrogen fluoride."

From *Teaching the Gifted Child*, by J. J. Gallagher (Boston: Allyn and Bacon, 1985), p. 10.

Maybe you've met people who seem compelled to tell you their IQ scores — whether or not you're interested.

Some parents of gifted kids spend a lot of time talking about (and comparing) their children's IQs. It's the modern-day equivalent of bragging about whose kid walked first, talked first, and got the best report card.

There's an IQ mystique that leads people who know theirs to set their expectations accordingly. A boy who learns that he has an IQ of 140 may begin to see himself as an intellectual superman, able to leap the forces of ignorance in a single bound. But if he finds out instead that his IQ hovers around a "mere" 117, he may decide that his potential is limited to being just a bit above average — smart enough to get by, but not to effect change or make a difference in the world.

How sad — either way.

We're acquainted with quite a few adults who don't *want* to know their IQs. They would rather not get caught up in the mystique, thanks anyway. As one said, "What if I found out that mine was higher than I thought? Would I be disappointed with my life so far? Or what if I learned it was lower than I hoped? Would I feel as if I had been fooling myself and everyone else?"

Interestingly, much of the sound and fury over IQ may signify a lot less than we think. Critics of IQ testing and scores cite plenty of good reasons to *de*-emphasize their importance. Here are three of the most convincing:

1. Test questions may have more than one correct response, depending on the test-taker's perspective.

For example, one asks you to eliminate the word that doesn't belong in this group: *cricket, football, billiards, hockey.*

In fact, each one can be eliminated. *Cricket* is the only one of the four of British origin. *Billiards* is the only one played indoors. *Football* is the only one whose object is *not* to put a ball into a net. And which type of *hockey* is meant, field or ice?

Thus, the *real* answer is "all of the above." Unfortunately, that isn't a response option.

Which raises an important point: Can you be *too* smart and think *too* deeply to score high on some IQ tests?

2. IQ tests discriminate against people from poor, minority, or disadvantaged backgrounds.

Many IQ tests have a high "verbal load" — that is, they require a good working knowledge of vocabulary, ideas, and situations that are part of life in white, middle-class, advantaged America, like:

▶ What is an *ocelot*?

▶ Compare and judge Truman Capote and Norman Mailer for their portrayal of the male figure in the novel.

Obviously, you're more likely to know what an ocelot is if you've been to a zoo or have a set of encyclopedias at your disposal. But what if you haven't, and what if you don't?

You may know quite a bit about Capote and Mailer. Or you may not, but if anyone asked, you could talk at length about the novels of Gabriel Garcia Marquez, which you've read in the original Spanish.

Have you ever thought to yourself, "I would have done better on that test if only my teacher had asked the right questions"?

3. IQ test results are often misinterpreted or misunderstood.

Some people have the mistaken notion that "better at" means "better than." That is, that persons with high IQs are somehow superior to those with lower scores.

This line of thinking isn't only false, it's unfair. And since IQ tests have, in the past, discriminated against certain ethnic and racial groups, it furthers the unrighteous causes of racism and prejudice.

Misplaced ideas about what IQ means have done considerable harm to gifted education. Opponents argue that kids who go to special programs are going to get big heads and think they're better than other kids. To put it politely, this is baloney. Except for the occasional nerd who thinks that he or she can do no wrong, gifted kids are as regular as anyone else. They want to be liked. They want to be respected. They want to have fun. They have no more propensity toward conceit than their peers.

It's time to stop relying on IQ to tell us whether someone is smart or not. And it's time to start looking at giftedness as more than a score.

The Test of Time

Is Howard Gardner right? Are there as many types of intelligence as there are areas of human activity?

And what about Robert Sternberg? Will his idea of intelligence as a set of highly specialized social skills ring true for future generations?

Who knows? At the moment, no one does. It will be our children and our children's children who will ultimately decide if our late-20th century notions of intelligence hold water or ooze goo. Yesterday's scientific facts are today's mumbo-jumbo, so who's to say that our descendants in the year 2325 won't look back on us and marvel at our ignorance?

Or perhaps our ideas will prove as valid as our instincts, and they'll withstand the toughest test of all, tougher even than the most high-level IQ test: the test of time.

"A man must have a certain amount of intelligent ignorance to get anywhere."
— *Charles Frank Kettering*

To find out more about intelligence, intelligences, and intelligence testing, read:

You're Smarter Than You Think, by Linda Perigo Moore (New York: Holt, Rinehart and Winston, 1985).

Frames of Mind: The Theory of Multiple Intelligences, by Howard Gardner (New York: Basic Books, Inc., 1983; paperback edition, New York: Harper & Row, 1985).

Beyond IQ: A Triarchic Theory of Human Intelligence, by Robert Sternberg (New Rochelle, NY: Cambridge University Press, 1984).

The Mismeasure of Man, by Stephen Jay Gould (New York: W. W. Norton & Co., 1981).

COUNTING YOUR BRAINS

There's been a lot of talk — and controversy — in recent years about the right brain vs. the left brain. Which is in charge? Which does what? If we do most of our thinking with one side, how can we learn to use the other? How can we achieve whole-brain learning?

The question about which side is in charge has given rise to the *cerebral dominance debate* (or *hemisphericity debate*), a hot topic among professionals these days. While in recent years researchers and scientists have discovered many things about that grayish blob between our ears, they often disagree with one another. It seems that for every study that documents one theory, there's another that contradicts it.

The concept of hemisphericity can be confusing — especially when some brain enthusiasts and pop psychologists misinterpret brain research. This can lead us to actually inhibit or limit our intellectual powers.

Some assessments claim to be able to identify the dominant side of the brain. You may have taken such an assessment in school. It may have suggested that you're "right-brained" or "left-brained." What's wrong with that? To begin with, it's much too simplistic. It's not enough to label a person one-brained or the other without providing some background information to put it all into perspective.

Otherwise, it's tempting to use one's brain label as an excuse for bad behavior or fear of trying something new.

G. Developing paper & chemicals (get from art department).

H. Typesetting for photo titles? (ask advisor of school paper).

I. Framing & matting materials (art department).

IV. **ROADBLOCKS:**

A. No one has ever done this sort of thing before (at least, not that I know of). Teacher may be reluctant to let me. ("Everybody else has to write about the poem, so why shouldn't you?") POSSIBLE SOLUTION: Arrange a conference with teacher to talk about poem. I'll be doing as much research as anyone else, just using it differently. Prove that I know about the poem & can discuss it intelligently. ALSO: Maybe see if other students in the class want to work on the photo essay with me, as a shared project? Then I won't be the only one doing something different.

The School Philosophy Statement allows for "creative development," "differentiated learning experiences," "student exploration," "individual independence," "artistic pursuits," and "challenge to reach potential." I think my project fits all of these.

B. I may not be allowed to use the stage. POSSIBLE SOLUTION: Set up "studio" in garage or basement.

C. Drama Club members may not want to be models. POSSIBLE SOLUTION: Ask friends — maybe kids from American Lit. class?

D. Drama Club, English department may not let me use costumes & props. POSSIBLE SOLUTION: Rent clothes from the Old-time Costume Emporium; rent props from Prop-Finders? (Or see if they'll let me borrow them for free if I give them credit?)

V. **REWARDS:**

A. Credit for doing the assignment.

B. A chance to show my photography somewhere outside the art department.

C. More experience working with live models.

D. Getting to know and work with kids from the Drama Club.

E. Becoming a better photographer.

F. Helping other kids to understand the poem better. (A picture is worth a thousand words!)

G. A great learning experience!

SIGNED:

_____   _____
Student   Teacher

_____   _____
DATE   DATE

"Let us go then, you and I,
When the evening is spread out against the sky
Like a patient etherized upon a table . . . "
— T. S. Eliot, from "The Love Song of J. Alfred Prufrock"

---

*"It has **finally** dawned on me that if the system won't change, it's up to me to make my classes more interesting. Now, as a result of learning to do things differently, I can honestly say school is really looking up! All the action feels good — I'm having fun. I've realized I have more opportunities and choices available to me than most kids. . . . All I have to do is to go get them."*

— Janice, 15

Assessing the Alternatives

Maybe you don't have to make changes in your school. Maybe several options and alternatives are already in place. *Maybe all you have to do is find out about them* and how you can take advantage of them.

A wide variety of possibilities exist at many schools across the country. Let's look at some of them.

Advanced Placement (A.P.) Classes. The College Board administers a set of college-level courses that are taught in many high schools. These A.P. courses often take a full year to complete, but since there's usually a greater emphasis on scholarship than on rote memorization, the work is more challenging.

A.P. courses are available in all regular school subjects, as well as computer science, foreign languages, music theory, studio art, and calculus (among others).

One of the biggest benefits of A.P. is that a successfully completed course and exam qualify you for college credit. Some students start college with a full semester of coursework earned through A.P. There is a charge — about $50 — for each A.P. exam, but in terms of potential college tuition saved, this is a wise investment, not just an expense.

Is your high school too small to offer A.P., or does it offer it only on a limited scale? No problem. If you're adept in calculus, for example, you may take the A.P. exam without having taken the A.P. calculus course. What a deal! And there are no age or grade restrictions on who can take the exams.

For more information about A.P., send for the no-cost "Guide to the Advanced Placement Program." Write: College Board Publication Orders, Box 886, New York, NY 10101. Or ask your school counselor about it; he or she may have a copy.

Weighted Grades and Transcripts. Many students are given the option of taking high school courses at the honors level. Although these aren't A.P. courses, their content and requirements may be equally rigorous.

Since you'll be asked to expend more effort in these classes, you ought to get more out of them. Like extra credit — literally. By taking harder courses, you'll be risking getting lower grades than if you took regular-track courses, so it's not unreasonable to expect something in return.

Ask your principal or guidance counselor what rewards exist for students who take honors-level courses. Often, an honors grade will be weighted — that is, a B or B + in Honors English will be noted on your transcript as being equivalent to an A in the nonhonors track.

At the very least, a notation should be made on your transcript indicating which courses you took at the honors level. College admission officers pay attention to this sort of thing.

One 15-year-old North Carolina student took up the issue of weighted grades at her high school. She researched the topic and found, among other things, that a California statute mandates that all honors courses statewide be weighted. Armed with this precedent and the support of several teachers and the PTA, she approached her local school board with a weighted grades proposal. The board accepted her recommendation.

A word of caution: Some people are against weighted grades, arguing that "bright students shouldn't *need* extra incentive to take harder courses." If you hear this line of unreasoning, stay calm. Try this response on for size: "Would *you* work overtime every day, without pay, just because you're a valued employee?" It *may* help to get your point across. Then again, it may not.

Early College Entrance. Remember David Huang, the 9-year-old college sophomore we introduced in the beginning of the book? To be sure, his case was unusual. But the option offered to enhance his education — early entrance to college — is a time-tested strategy that's available to many gifted high school students.

It usually works in one of two ways:

1. You do well enough in your freshman through junior years to apply early to a college of your choice. If you show strong promise (high grades and ACT/SAT scores), many colleges will consider accepting you as a full-time student at the end of your

junior year. Check with the colleges you're interested in to see if they allow for this option, called "early admission."

2. The "dual enrollment" option allows you to take college courses at a local university while you're attending high school. It works best when you live near a college campus and transportation between the two schools isn't a problem. Even if the nearest college is 100 miles away, you may be able to take summer courses to build up your academic credentials (and have more fun).

Adults seem to prefer the second option over the first. They believe that it's important for high school students to be able to participate in high school social events — proms, pep rallies, yearbook committees, clubs, and the like.

They have a point. It *is* easier to make up for lost time in academics than in dating and other forms of social development. On the other hand, some high school students could care less about football, dances, homecoming floats, and the like. That's why each decision must be made on an individual basis. When it comes to planning academic futures, there's no such thing as "one size fits all."

"There's more learning than is taught in books."
— Lady Gregory

CAN HIGH SCHOOL STUDENTS SUCCEED IN COLLEGE CLASSES?

In one Midwestern state, the answer seems to be a big YES.

In 1985–1986, high school juniors and seniors in Minnesota had the chance to participate in the Post Secondary Options Program. They could enroll free for classes in colleges, universities, and technical schools and earn high school and college credits.

Over 3,500 students signed up. When the Minnesota Department of Education surveyed 1,000 of these students, here's what they found:

- ▶ Students completed nearly 87 percent of the courses and failed less than 1 percent.

- ▶ 52 percent of the grades earned by 11th- and 12th-graders were A's or B's.

- ▶ 95 percent of the students said that they were "satisfied" or "very satisfied" with the experience.

- ▶ More than 80 percent said that the experience helped prepare them for college.

- ▶ 90 percent said that they learned more by participating in the program than they would have if they had taken only high school courses.

The Smorgasbord Approach. There's no rule that says you must try honors courses *or* A.P. *or* early admission *or* dual enrollment. If you can't make up your mind about which is the best option for you, then perhaps you can decide not to decide.

You don't have to do anything. Or you can do a little bit of everything, trying bits and pieces of each program that appeals to you.

For example, you might register for three A.P. classes and, at the same time, contact colleges about transferring the credits you earn. Couple this request with a query about their summer enrollment policies for qualified high school students, and you may be on your way to designing an educational program that fits you like a glove.

HOW TO WRITE TO A COLLEGE ADMISSIONS OFFICE

The following letter was written by an actual high school student to an actual college admissions office. (The student's name and address have been changed, but the letter is word-for-word, otherwise.)

Beverly Michaels
123 Collegebound Way
Albany, NY 13524

Honors College
Kent State University
Kent, Ohio 44242

Admissions Office:

My name is Beverly Michaels, and I am very interested in attending your school. At the present time I am a junior at Hudson Valley High School. I would like to know if you could possibly send me any information on your Early Admissions Program.

In the past year, I have moved around quite a bit and my grades have fluctuated, but I am very ambitious and I am trying very hard to get them back on the right track. I have taken all the college bound courses that your school requires, but I still have to complete 2 or 3 classes in order to meet my high school's requirements for graduation. I will be taking my SAT's and ACT's in March or April. I will have those scores sent to you immediately.

I don't want to spend a year in high school just for 3 classes. I believe it would be a wasted year and I would rather be meeting a challenge and using my ability to learn new and important things.

Please get back to me as quickly as possible. Thank you.

Sincerely,

Beverly Michaels

Improving Your Attitude

If you really want to become an effective change agent for your own education, you need one more important tool: **a good attitude.** Teachers and administrators aren't going to bend over backwards to please you if you come on like Genghis Khan.

First and foremost, you should communicate an attitude of cooperation, not condescension. Set yourself up as an ally, not an aggressor. Most teachers want to help their students; that's one reason they've chosen the teaching profession. Acknowledge that, respect it, make it easier for them to work with you, and the rewards will be substantial.

There's nothing better than having your teachers on your side. And it's not that hard to enlist their aid. All it takes is a dash of diplomacy and the willingness to recognize that teachers are people, too.

Consider the following — and notice the difference in each approach to the same problem.

Condescension	Cooperation
"This class is B-O-R-I-N-G! I'm not learning anything."	"I already learned most of this last year. Can I prove that I know it by taking a test or completing a special project?"
"I HATE it when you give me an A and don't tell me what you liked about my work."	"I'd appreciate knowing what it was about my project that made you think it deserved an A. Can you give me some specifics?"
"It really stinks that just because I'm gifted, you expect me to always get top grades."	"I'm better at some things than others. I don't want to be #1 all the time at everything."

"You always say, 'I have 100 students a day; how can I individualize for you?' What a cop-out!"

"I've come up with some ideas for completing my course requirements in a different way than usual. Can I talk to you about them?"

As an *aggressor*, you set up a situation where someone will win and someone will lose; the battle lines are drawn, and there's no going back. As an *ally*, you don't accuse your teacher of doing a poor job or disregarding your needs and emotions. Instead, you state very clearly and directly, "Here's what's going on, here's how I feel about it, and this is what I'd like to do instead."

A 7th-grader from Texas told us this story: It seems that one of her teachers was alienating his students by constantly stressing the negative. "No matter what we did, it wasn't good enough," she says. "Even if the whole class did well on a test, he'd pick on the one idea we missed. He was really making us hate his class!"

One day she walked up to him and said, "When you tell me everything I do is wrong, it makes me feel dumb. You make me feel like I'll *never* be successful."

How did her teacher respond? "He said he had no idea what a negative effect he was having," the student recalls. "He said he thought his approach would make us want to work harder. He actually *thanked* me for being so honest!"

Did she take a risk? You bet. Did it pay off? You decide. Would she do it again? Very philosophically, she states, "If I thought my gripe was legitimate, yes, I would. Also, what did I have to lose? The class couldn't have gotten any worse, so the only way to go was up!"

Granted, you won't always achieve your objective, no matter what approach you choose. Some teachers, unfortunately, think they have to act as aggressors toward their students. But you're much more likely to be heard if you put aside the verbal boxing gloves and come out smiling.

TO GT OR NOT TO GT?

Many gifted students have a problem that can't be solved by asserting their rights, exploring alternatives, or even being nice to their teachers. It has to do with the fact that there's more to life than school.

If you're in a special program for gifted and talented students, you may find that it takes up an awful lot of your time. Too much, in fact. Especially if you're also involved in other things — like sports, school clubs or organizations, and the pursuit of a healthy social life. And what if you also have an after-school job? Chores to do around the house? Plus the occasional need to eat and sleep?

What it might boil down to is the question, "To GT or not to GT?" Is it worth it to you to stay in the gifted/talented program?

That's something only **you** can decide. And a good way to approach this decision is to list all the activities you're involved in (and have some control over) and then rank them according to how important they are to **you**.

Jerry, 15, came up with this list:

> Track team
> Part-time job
> Stock market club
> G/T independent study group
> Scouts
> Computer games
> Goofing off

When he was through ranking the items, it looked like this:

2. Track team
1. Part-time job

6. Stock market club
5. G/T independent study group
3. Scouts
4. Computer games
7. Goofing off

Jerry needed his part-time job to earn money for college — plus, he liked it and the people he worked with. He'd been on the track team for years and was hoping, in fact, that his talents in that area might help him get a college scholarship. He'd been in scouts since he was a little kid and wasn't about to give that up. And his great joy in life — aside from track and scouting — was playing computer games. That put his G/T independent study group at #5, pretty low on the list.

After you've made your list and assigned each item a number, put it away for a week to 10 days and don't look at it. Then create a new list with new rankings, take out your first list, and compare the two. Activities low on both lists may be ripe for reevaluating and perhaps cutting out of your life.

Your decisions don't have to be etched in stone. You may decide that working on the school paper is too demanding now, and then choose to go back to it next term or next year. You may want to take a temporary leave from the karate club, with the option of joining up again in a month or two. And you may determine that the honors program in English isn't worth the effort, but the honors program in math is.

Circumstances change, people change, priorities and interests change. You may need to reassess and realign your options at a later date, depending on who you are by then.

Don't feel as if you have to apologize for your choices. Whatever activities you decide to curtail — be it the swim team or the G/T program — there will probably be people (teachers, coaches, advisors, or parents) who may try to convince you to change your mind. Especially if they have made a personal investment in you and your performance. Hear them out respectfully and weigh their arguments carefully, but remember that the final decision is yours.

VOICES OF EXPERIENCE

Sometimes, it feels as if you're the only person who has ever had problems dealing with school. As if no one else could possibly understand. As if you're all alone on a mountain-top, looking out at the landscape and wondering what the heck is going on.

In fact, you have a lot in common with our nation's most creative writers, scientists, lawyers, and artists. Some of them had a tough time in school. Some of them had to figure out their own ways of dealing with the pressures, the frustrations, and the occasional in-anities involved in getting a decent education. Many of them felt like loners, too.

A book called *Educating Able Learners*, by J. Cox, N. Daniel, and B. Boston, reports on this group of winners. Maybe you've heard of the MacArthur Fellows, gifted adults ages 20–80 who receive any-where from $20,000–$60,000 per year for five years, no strings at-tached. All are selected on the basis of past accomplishments and awarded the money in the belief that it will free them to devote more time to their chosen areas of expertise.

Here's what some MacArthur Fellows have to say about their years in school:

"My grades were adequate, but I hated the pressure and high level of competition. For example, in my math class, the seating was rearranged after every test, with the highest average in the right front, the lowest in the left rear . . . an enormous premium [was] placed on grades."

— Geologist, 38

"Achieving in school per se didn't mean anything to me. I think I had an innate feeling that one was obligated to do at least the minimum work required so as not to create problems for oneself or others, but I never realized that what I considered to be the minimum was often far more than it was for others."
— Historian, 31

"I was very active in school, partly to overcome the negative connotations of being an egghead."
— Historian, 40

"Certainly I've always learned more out of school than in."
— Biochemist, 28

It sounds as if school wasn't all that different for them than it is for bright kids today. In fact, the MacArthur Fellows would probably agree with these Three Great Truths of Getting an Education:

1. Teachers *can* help, if you give them a chance.
2. No situation is perfect, and some educators and students are overtly antagonistic toward gifted kids.
3. If you expect learning to happen to you — like an accident or a suntan — you'll end up learning only what others want you to learn.

The last point may be the most important of all. Ultimately, you're the one who has to decide whether to learn only what you must, or to take advantage of all the opportunities and options available to you.

INGREDIENTS FOR SUCCESS

hat personal traits make for a successful school experience? The achieving students we interviewed seemed to have these characteristics in common:

▶ They perceived themselves as competent, capable people.
▶ They were able to accomplish tasks without undue tension or stress.
▶ They believed that *they* were responsible for their own performance. They didn't blame others when they did poorly (for example, "I've got a lousy teacher"), nor did they credit others for their achievements ("I got an A because the teacher likes me").
▶ They thought school was important but not *all*-important. They gave themselves time and room to enjoy other, more social aspects of growing up.
▶ They understood and accepted that school isn't always 100 percent fulfilling. It can be boring. It can be maddening. It can be blah. But that's all part of the package.
▶ They didn't see themselves as failures if they achieved less than perfection, nor did they place an overwhelming emphasis on mistakes.

The distinction between success and failure is a highly personal one. For someone who typically performs at a C level, a grade of B seems outstanding. But for someone used to getting A's, a B is a real blow. Again, it's up to you to decide how good is good enough, how high is high enough, and what it's worth to you.

"Success is important only to the extent that it puts one in a position to do more things one likes to do."
— *Sarah Caldwell*

To find out more about what school should or could be like for gifted and talented students, read:

Educating Able Learners, by J. Cox, N. Daniel, and B. Boston (Austin, TX: University of Texas Press, 1985).

Developing Talent in Young People, edited by Benjamin S. Bloom (New York: Ballantine Books, 1985).

WHOSE LIFE IS IT, ANYWAY?

It's common for gifted kids to be recognized by their parents. Not in the sense of "Hey! I know you! You look like me!" but acknowledged as being just a little different from other youngsters.

For example, if you started reading billboards, cereal boxes, and road signs when you were 3 years old, your folks might have suspected that you were precocious. Likewise, if your computer has long been your most treasured possession, chess your preferred spectator sport, or the evening news your favorite TV program, your parents might have surmised that your intellectual talents were out of the ordinary. (Of course, you may also have enjoyed baseball, tree climbing, and Saturday morning cartoons; gifted kids aren't limited to intellectual pursuits alone.)

But let's say that your abilities became evident long before you entered kindergarten. There were probably folks around you — parents, grandparents, neighbors — who found it hard to disguise their pride.

If even one member of your family has decided that you're the one who will "make us proud," and if everyone (except you) seems to know which career you should choose, then you'll probably identify with the 16-year-old who said:

> "Being gifted, I have a strong sense of future, because people are always telling me how well I will do when I grow up. . . . My feelings fluctuate from a sense of respon-

sibility for everything to a kind of 'leave me alone, quit pushing.' "

From *On Being Gifted* (New York: American Association for Gifted Children/ Walker & Co., 1977), p. 7.

Ambition and drive are commendable traits. Expectations aren't bad, either, since they provide a goal or two to strive for. But if you're a gifted teenager, they can combine to create a list of demands that are difficult to meet.

Adding to the confusion is the sad fact that the harder you try to please adults, the easier it is to turn off your friends. You've heard the names kids call one another (and maybe you've been on the receiving end): "teacher's pet," "brown nose," "Mama's boy (or girl)."

So, what's the answer? Should you defer to adults who insist on planning your future? Should you turn a deaf ear to all advice? Should you start doing less than you're capable of, hoping that the grown-ups in your life will lower their estimation of your talents and your peers will accept you more readily?

Sometimes, it seems as if there are too many choices to make. And each carries its own set of drawbacks and rewards.

MULTIPOTENTIAL: AN EMBARRASSMENT OF RICHES

C harlie Brown, speaking to Linus on the meaning of life, once lamented, "There is no heavier burden than a great potential." For when you are bright and good at a lot of different things, it becomes very easy to disappoint those people who have your future all planned out.

Perhaps Mom has always wanted you to be a doctor, while Dad has dreams of your taking over the family business. Your high school chemistry teacher might be pushing you toward a degree at M.I.T., while the school counselor is urging you toward Harvard or Yale. And if you're female, you may even be hearing from well-intentioned (but old-fashioned) relatives that finding a husband should be your primary goal.

What to be? What to become? Where to go? Where to turn? And how to convince everyone to let you make up your *own* mind?

For more than 30 years, researchers at the University of Wisconsin have studied the problems encountered by gifted teens seeking answers to career-related questions. They have used interviews, questionnaires, and follow-up surveys with hundreds of young adults in the hopes of clearing up some of the fuzzier facets of career selection and satisfaction.

One of their most important findings is this: Gifted teenagers are often interested in — and have the potential to succeed at — a whole slew of career options. The experts at the U of Wisconsin have labeled this characteristic *multipotential.*

75

In describing his multipotential, 17-year-old Mike said:

> "I participated in three semesters of a mentorship pro-
> gram. In one placement I worked with a physician who
> does research at the university. In a second setting I
> worked with an attorney, and in the third a computer ex-
> pert. I had great experience in all three settings and felt
> like I could be successful in any of those professions. I
> guess I'm not any closer to knowing what I want to do in
> the future. Maybe I'll have to figure out a way to combine
> all three of those areas into a 'custom designed' job."

While it sounds wonderful, multipotential can be a burden — but
let's face it, complaining about it won't elicit much sympathy from
others. "I'm so good at so many things that I just can't make up my
mind" is not the sort of comment that will win friends and influence
people.

It helps to know that you're not alone. The dilemma posed by multipotential is shared by many gifted persons.

> *"I ended up teaching at a university, but not until I'd toyed with the
> fields of psychiatry, pediatrics, and forestry."*
> — Jim, 33

> *"I got my B.A. in psychology, worked for an orchestra, went to busi-
> ness school for my M.B.A., and now I'm vice president of a software
> company. I may have arrived by an indirect route, but I like where
> I am."*
> — Leah, 36

> *"I work in advertising, I enjoy it, and I'm good at it, but I also take
> flying lessons on the weekends and I wonder — is it too late to ap-
> ply to astronaut school?"*
> — Tania, 30

Multipotential is a mixed blessing, to be sure. But recognizing it is a
step in the direction of living with it — and making the most of it.

Even when you do decide on a career, you don't have to stick with it forever. Lots of people switch careers once, twice, and even more often before they retire — going back to school for degrees in other fields, changing companies, starting their own businesses.

Multipotential may mean occasional headaches. But it also means *choices* — enough for a lifetime.

What's the Secret to Success? Making *informed* choices.

"When I think of the hundreds of things I might be, I get down on my knees and thank God that I'm me."
— Elsie Janis

Making Informed Choices

What do **you** want to be when you grow up? If you can't answer, don't worry. Plenty of adults in their 30s, 40s, 50s, and beyond are still wrestling with this question.

But let's say you have a general idea of the direction you think your life should take. For example, you've assessed your talents and abilities and have some notion of what you're cut out to be. The point is not to specialize early or sign up only for those courses that fit with your eventual goal but to *find out as much as you can about what it will take to get there.*

What do you need to learn? do? become? Which people you should talk to? Which colleges or universities should you start thinking about? What will you need to do to put your plan into action? When should you begin?

Following are some time-tested techniques for you to try.

Touch before you tackle.

Often, when deciding on a college major or a career focus, gifted teens make up their minds too soon.

"I was sure from the day I started high school that I wanted to be an English teacher. All the way through college, I took as many English courses as I could and the bare minimum in all other subject areas. The summer before I was supposed to go to graduate school, I got a part-time job at a bank. I liked it so much that I never left. Five years later, I wish I knew more about math and economics."
— Andrew, 26

"If I had it to do over, I'd probably take courses in art history, philosophy, and music — subjects I neglected because I was sure I wanted to be a doctor. I got on the premed track too soon, and now I wish I had studied other subjects in more depth."
— Gina, 30

Let's say you're 14 and want to be an allergist someday. Ask yourself: What is it about that particular profession that interests you? The money? the prestige? the independence? the challenge? A career as an allergist is nothing to sneeze at; how thoroughly have you examined the pros and cons? What kind of investment are you willing to make to meet your goal? Can you see spending more than eight years in college and $50,000-plus in tuition costs and loans? What is an allergist's life really like?

It's not hard to find the answers to these questions and more. Our society is full of specialists, and there's bound to be at least one who's willing to talk to you.

Think about it: If a kid on the brink of 7th grade walked up to you and said, "Come on, tell me a little bit about junior high — what's it *really* like?" wouldn't you be flattered? And wouldn't you be willing to describe the ins and outs of food fights, jammed lockers, and getting along with teachers?

It's the same with adults. Most of us enjoy talking about ourselves and our experiences, especially to people who are seriously interested in what we have to say. You may want to conduct several fact-finding interviews.

Or consider an internship, if available. Many businesses offer them during the summer and part-time during the school year. An internship gives you the chance to "try on" a profession without making a commitment. It may not pay much in terms of dollars, but it will give you experiences and insights you can't buy.

"I'm not sure I want to be a vampire, so I'm doing a summer internship at the local blood bank . . . If it drives me batty I'll go into something else."

To find out about more than 30,000 internships for high school students, read:

Internships, edited by Katherine Jobst (Cincinnati, OH: Writer's Digest Books, 1987).

Consider creating your own career.

If early specializers are at one end of the spectrum, the opposite end is crowded with people who can't make up their minds.

You've probably met someone — you may *be* someone — who wants to be everything: psychologist, rock star, architect, poet, boutique owner, missionary, frozen-foods distributor, engineer, pilot. Trying to fulfill *just one* of these ambitions seems as silly as going to a smorgasbord and eating only mashed potatoes. The selections are so varied and look so appealing that you want a little taste of each.

Many gifted persons who fit this description decide to focus on one career for a while and use their free time to explore other options.

"Right now I'm teaching courses in special ed while taking courses in archaeology. This summer I'll go on a dig to Mexico as part of my master's degree program."
— Ron, 28

"I couldn't choose between careers in medicine and art; I enjoy both areas. So I'm studying both in the hope of becoming a medical artist for anatomy textbooks."
— Therese, 19

These two individuals have "married" their vocations with their avocations. And each is in process of creating a career, rather than fitting in to preexisting ones.

If your multipotential has you confused about what to do and be, ask yourself these two questions:

1. What would you **like** to be doing ten years from now?

2. What do you **think** you'll be doing ten years from now?

If your responses differ (and they probably will), sit down and consider how you can mesh them into a future of your own devising. It's not that uncommon these days to strike out on one's own. More and more people are choosing the entrepreneurial route — starting their own companies, inventing their own jobs. Countless occupations exist today that weren't even imagined a decade ago. Why not add to the list?

"The ablest man I ever met is the man you think you are."
— Franklin D. Roosevelt

You'll doubtless encounter a few people who will urge you to quit goofing off and get down to business. And at times, you may question the validity of your decision, especially since you may not have much company along your eclectic way. Don't be diverted by the doubters or the self-doubts. Times change, needs change, and **you** will change, too. With the right blend of gumption and drive, you may find yourself shifting directions several times before you're ready to retire.

In other words, a career choice doesn't have to be a life sentence.

*"I've spent the past 11 years as a freelance writer, and it's only been in the last year or so that my parents have stopped asking me, 'When are you going to get a **real** job?'"*
— Marybeth, 32

*"My parents and my brothers and sisters all work 9-to-5 jobs. I think they resent it that I have my own business and don't work for anyone else. What they don't realize is that I put in 12 and sometimes 14 hours a day. The big difference is, I work for **me**."*
— Dexter, 25

Explore the road less traveled.

To choose the "road less traveled" (as Robert Frost wrote) or to "bravely go where no man has gone before" (in the words of Captain Kirk) is to leave yourself open to criticism and a chorus of "I-told-you-so's" in the event of a setback or failure. But if your reason for selecting pottery or nursing over podiatry or nuclear physics stems from your own genuine interest and belief that it's right for **you**, that's all **you** need to heed.

"Two roads diverged in a wood, and I — I took the one less traveled by, And that has made all the difference."
— Robert Frost

Listen to what Colin (who grade-skipped his way to a Ph.D. at 21, then went on to be a college professor of economics) has to say:

> "The only thing people can rightfully demand from you is excellence — or at least an honest effort — in whatever you decide to do, whether it is ballet, engineering, economics, or rock music. In fact, the only reason you owe excellence in exchange for your gift is that you owe it *to yourself*. . . .'That's impossible' and 'That's too wild an idea' are the favorite chants of the narrow minded."

From *Gifted Children Speak Out*, by James R. Delisle (New York: Walker & Co., 1984).

And listen to Rick DeFuria, a Sarasota County, Florida judge who gave up his $60,000-a-year job to pursue his lifelong dream of being an actor:

> "Frankly, I became bored. I was trying to find something more stimulating. . . .I could be the biggest disaster in the world. But to have gone through life and never tried would have been a tragedy. And if it doesn't work, well, there's always law."

From the *Los Angeles Times*, September 30, 1986.

"Adventure is worthwhile in itself."
— Amelia Earhart

To find out more about making career choices, read:

What To Be, by V. Weiss and S. Berman (Englewood Cliffs, NJ: Prentice-Hall, 1981).

Working, by Studs Terkel (New York: Ballantine Books, 1985, pbk.).

CAUTION: If *Working* was a movie, it would be rated R for language. If you don't mind the strong stuff, it's well worth reading.

NATTERING NABOBS OF NEGATIVISM

I n addition to people who try to plan your future, there will also be those who attempt to put a damper on your present.

Maybe you already know one or more Nattering Nabobs of Negativism. These are the people who let you know, in ways both subtle and direct, that you aren't as smart, good looking, ambitious, or whatever as you would like to believe you are.

NNNs specialize in putting people down. They look and sound sincere and swear to have your best interests at heart as they say things like:

- *"I'm sure you'll do fine at State College. Those Ivy League schools are much too expensive anyway, and besides, you have to be **really** smart to get into Brown or Vassar."*

- *"How nice that you want to get your Ph.D. in archaeology. But didn't you once want to become an M.D. — you know, the kind of doctor who helps people?"*

- *"It's just fine with me if you want to go to law school. I hope that C you got in your junior high social studies class won't hold you back."*

- *"You're a talented actor, no question about that. But are you sure you want to make a career of it? Can you stand all those years of rejection?"*

Get the picture? NNNs somehow manage to make you feel like a million bucks — after taxes. Every compliment comes with a reminder that all is not well; that with just a little more effort, you might have been a *real* success. Their favorite word is **but.**

If you allow it to happen, the NNNs of the world will get to you. They'll convince you that your accomplishments are meager and your pursuits just shy of trivial.

Don't let them! They can natter, nag, and make nuisances of themselves, but what you ultimately do is up to you.

"No one can make you feel inferior without your consent."

— *Eleanor Roosevelt*

TAKING CHARGE OF YOUR LIFE

Unless your career goal is to be a hermit, you probably can't escape from the planners, prodders, and Nattering Nabobs in your life. Parents, teachers, friends, neighbors, siblings, and strangers will keep trying to tell you what (and what not) to do with all that potential you have.

Listen politely, smile, and take some comfort in the fact that most of them mean well. Just remember that they can't run your life — unless you let them.

How can you improve your chances of getting where you want to go? *By setting realistic expectations for yourself.*

Setting Realistic Expectations

As hard as others can be on you, chances are you're even harder on yourself. Expectations can creep up on you as slowly but surely as barnacles on a barge.

Are you ever satisfied with being adequate? With just doing okay on a test instead of getting an A? Do you ever do the minimum that's required of you? Are you comfortable with an occasional failure?

If you answered *no* to all of the above, you may be suffering from *perfectionism.*

Psychologists and educators have long argued about how and where perfectionism begins. Is it self-inflicted (do perfectionists choose to be that way) or other-inflicted (are they made that way by parents, teachers, etc.)? Whatever its source, perfectionism can be a major roadblock on your way to success and peace of mind.

If you can never settle for anything less than first place, you're in for a lot of disappointment. Perfection simply isn't possible. And even when you do reach the top, you may find that holding on isn't worth the effort.

"If I don't get a perfect test score, my parents make a big deal out of it. Sometimes I wish I could go back to first grade and start over. I'd never get an A!"
— Dinah, 13

"There isn't really anyone else to compete with, so I compete against myself. And I'm hardly ever happy with my own performance."
— Terry, 15

Another problem perfectionists have is the tendency to pooh-pooh past accomplishments.

"I'm proud of the things I do when I do them, but when I look back at them later, they seem mediocre. I always tell myself 'You could have done better if you'd just tried harder.' "
— Jennifer, 16

Fortunately, there's a cure for perfectionism. What it takes is the ability to put things into perspective. For example:

▶ You see yourself as an A student — until the day you get your first B+. You're shocked. You're stunned. You're furious with yourself.

But wait: What did you get that B+ in? Rotation Biology II? Advanced Placement Medieval Literature? A course in which all the material was brand new to you? It *does* make a difference.

MacArthur Fellow quotes from *Educating Able Learners: Programs and Promising Practices*, by J. Cox, N. Daniel, and B. Boston (Austin, TX: University of Texas Press, 1985). Copyright ©1985 by the University of Texas Press. Reprinted by permission.

> "Take one a day for the rest of your life."

▶ For years, everyone has been telling you what a terrific athlete you are. You start high school expecting to win a letter in every sport you participate in, from football to jujitsu.

But wait: Do you know any athletes who are good at everything? Even those who get as far as the Olympics tend to specialize in only one sport. Have you ever heard of an ice skater who was also a sumo wrestler? Or a championship swimmer who went from the pool to the basketball court with equal ease?

▶ You're nominated to run for Student Council President — and you lose. You feel dejected, rejected, and embarrassed.

But wait: Out of the dozens or even hundreds of students in your class, you *were* among the two or three whose names appeared on the ballot. That's something to be proud of. There's a *big* difference between thinking "I lost" and telling yourself "I came in second (or third)."

It's all a matter of attitude. What's yours? Do you tend to look on the dark side of everything, or are you one of those individuals who can see the sun shining through the thickest clouds?

ATTITUDE ADJUSTMENT QUIZ

1. This glass is

    a) half empty
    b) half full

2. This sky is

    a) partly cloudy
    b) partly sunny

3. This man is

    a) half bald
    b) half hairy

4. Your favorite ending for the word *hope* is

    a) *-less*
    b) *-ful*

5. At middle age, life is

    a) half gone
    b) half begun

SCORING:
Give yourself 1 point for every "a" answer, and no points for every "b" answer.

INTERPRETING YOUR SCORE:
0–1: An Eternal Optimist, you see everything and everyone in a positive light. To you, a hurricane is an opportunity to blow-dry your hair.

2–3: A Realist, you're always weighing pros and cons. And you're hesitant to take things or people at face value.

4–5: An Eternal Pessimist, you see everything and everyone in a negative light. If you won a brand-new Corvette, you'd probably complain about the color. Lighten up!

Fortunately, there is a healthy alternative to perfectionism. It's called the Pursuit of Excellence. Here are some ways they differ:

Perfectionism means thinking less of yourself because you got a B+ instead of an A.

The Pursuit of Excellence means thinking more of yourself for trying something new.

Perfectionism means being hard on yourself because you aren't equally talented in all sports.

The Pursuit of Excellence means choosing some things you know you'll be good at — and others you know will be good for you or just plain fun.

Perfectionism means feeling rotten because you lost the student council election.

The Pursuit of Excellence means patting yourself on the back because you were nominated. And deciding to run again next year — if that's what you want.

How can you become a Pursuer of Excellence? By . . .

. . . uncovering the sources of your perfectionism,
. . . reassessing your feelings about failure, and
. . . defending yourself against people who pressure you to be perfect.

▶ Uncovering the sources of your perfectionism.

Maybe your parents are always pushing you to stay at the head of your class. Maybe your teachers are always reminding you to "keep up the good work." Maybe your classmates are always saying things like "We know you'll win the district essay contest. Go get 'em!" And maybe you're always telling yourself that first place is the only place worth being.

Any and all of these influences can drive you to perfectionism. In fact, it may seem as if you don't have any choice. What's the price you pay for *not* being perfect? You risk disappointing everyone around you — and yourself.

It's great when your parents and teachers and classmates are behind you. It's terrific when they believe in you. It's wonderful if you have confidence in yourself. But any and all of these can be carried too far. When that happens, you're the one who suffers. Some of the effects of perfectionism include anxiety, stress, poor health, "brain paralysis," and burnout.

Who are the people in your life who seem to want you to be perfect? Who are the people who like and accept you just as you are?

▶ **Reassessing your feelings about failure.**

Gifted kids often have special problems with perfectionism. They're constantly driven to compete, perform, and excel. To them, fail is a four-letter word.

The truth is, **nobody's perfect.** The successful people in the world know this. They're the ones who have figured out how to live with failure, take it in stride, and learn from it. They realize that the road to achievement is paved with mistakes. They trip over them, pick themselves up, and move on.

How do *you* feel when your performance is less than flawless? What can you say to yourself the next time you fail at something? How can you develop a healthier, more positive attitude toward the possibility — and the reality — of failure?

"Be bold. If you're going to make an error, make a doozy, and don't be afraid to hit the ball."

— *Billie Jean King*

EIGHT NOTABLE FAILURES

- **Whoopi Goldberg** was a high school dropout.

- So was **Bill Cosby** — even though he had been assigned to a class for gifted students.

- **Billy Joel** once considered suicide and was quoted as saying, "The last thing the world needs is another failed artist."

- **Lee Iacocca** was fired from the Ford Motor Company.

- **Babe Ruth** struck out 1,330 times.

- By the tender age of 37, **Charles Post** was ill and had lost nearly all of his money in a land-development scheme. He went on to found Post Cereals.

- **William Wrigley, Jr.** was known as the "class bad boy" and was expelled after throwing a pie at the nameplate over the entrance to his school. In spite of his rough start in life, Wrigley's namesake chewing gum is known worldwide.

- After five failed attempts, **Annie Smith Peck** was (and still is) the only woman to make a first ascent of Huascaran in Lima, Peru — one of the world's major mountains.

▶ **Defending yourself against people who pressure you to be perfect.**

"I usually win a prize in our school science fair. But this year I was busy with a lot of other things and didn't spend as much time on my project. All my science teacher said was, 'What happened? You usually do such a great job.'"
— Kevin, 14

"My friends are always asking me for help with their homework. They act as if I always know everything, and when I say I don't know something, they think it's because I don't want to help them."
— Danetta, 12

"Whenever I don't do something perfectly, my mom says I'm wasting my abilities."
— Kim, 13

"Even my grandparents bug me about being gifted. Whenever I see them, the first thing they say is, 'How's our smartest grandchild?' I know they're proud of me, but it drives me crazy!"
— Charles, 15

There are times when brains can be a burden. When all around you people are telling you how smart you are — and how smart you'd better keep being. Usually they mean well, but so what? You want them to BUG OFF!

It's okay to tell them how you feel. It helps if you do it diplomatically. Here are a few short "speeches" you may want to practice, just to get the hang of it.

To your parents:

"I know you like it when I get straight A's. But I need you to understand that I worked just as hard for that B in Russian — maybe harder."
"I probably could have gotten an A in regular biology, but we all agreed that I should try the honors course. I think I'm learning a lot, and I want to stay in it. I need your support."

To your teachers:

"It bothers me that you're always calling on me and expecting me to know the answers. I feel pressured to perform all the time."
"Your ancient history course is a lot tougher than I thought it would be. I think it's worth the effort, but I wish you would stop expecting me to be the star student."

To your friends:

"Just because I'm a good student doesn't mean I spend my weekends with my nose in a book."
"Okay, so I get good grades. Big deal. Let's go shoot some baskets or something."

Be assertive, not aggressive; honest, not ornery. Most of the people who are pressuring you probably aren't aware of how you feel.

If you need extra help, arrange to talk to your school counselor. Explain what you're up against, and ask for suggestions. He or she should also be able to give you some sound advice or at least a few pointers in the right direction.

▼▼

To find out more about perfectionism, read:

Perfectionism: What's Bad About Being Too Good, by Miriam Adderholdt-Elliott (Minneapolis: Free Spirit Publishing, 1987).

Understanding Success and Failure, by Lois Roets (New Sharon, IA: Leadership Publications, 1985).

▲▲

Getting Sexism Out of the Way

How many househusbands do you know? What about male nurses? How many state governors are women? How many chief executive officers of major companies wear skirts to work?

People *talk* about how our society is becoming less sexist. In fact, it is — but it's a long, tedious process that frequently slows and stalls.

We may be a generation behind the time when a woman's place was strictly in the home and men provided the family's sole financial support, but sexism still permeates our culture and affects both males and females who deviate from certain prescribed roles.

"I do not believe in sex distinction in literature, law, politics, or trade — or that modesty and virtue are more becoming to women than to men, but wish we had more of it everywhere."
— *Belva Lockwood*

Psychologist Barbara Kerr, author of *Smart Girls, Gifted Women*, specializes in guidance for gifted females. In researching the attitudes and ambitions of gifted teenage girls, she has found some disturbing patterns.

▶ Gifted girls have higher career goals for themselves during childhood than they do during adolescence.

▶ They often lower their aspirations for academic achievement once they enter junior high school.

▶ When Lewis M. Terman (remember him?) retested the IQs of his test subject six years after beginning his study, he found that the boys' had dropped an average of 3 points, while the girls' had dropped an average of *13* points.

▶ Gifted teenage girls appear to be much more sensitive to social and societal criticism than boys and may be more likely to downplay their academic talents in order to be accepted by their classmates.

In her book, Kerr suggests ways that gifted girls can sustain their dreams over time — and ways that parents and teachers can help. She maintains that gifted females need special guidance and encouragement to believe that it's okay to be both feminine and competent and to enjoy algebra and chemistry, as well as dating and sports.

FROM GIFTED GIRLS TO EMINENT WOMEN:
11 Factors that Make a Difference

Barbara Kerr analyzed the lives of several eminent women in an attempt to learn how they managed to transcend the barriers to achievement that gifted women face. She found that scientist Marie Curie, writer Gertrude Stein, human rights activist Eleanor Roosevelt, anthropologist Margaret Mead, painter Georgia O'Keefe, writer, dancer, and political activist Maya Angelou, and singer Beverly Sills had all or most of these factors in common:

1. As girls, they spent time alone, whether by choice or necessity.

2. They read voraciously.

3. They felt "different" or "special."

4. They received individualized instruction as children, often in their areas of future fame.

5. They experienced embarrassing social awkwardness in adolescence.

6. Rather than defining themselves in terms of their relationships with others, they had a unique sense of self.

7. They took responsibility for themselves and their own lives.

8. They had the ability to fall in love with an idea; they had the capacity to be intensely interested in something and pursue it wholeheartedly.

9. They refused to acknowledge limitations of gender.

10. They had mentors — men or women who nurtured their talents and provided them access to a profession.

11. They were able to integrate several tasks and roles — wife, mother, career woman, leader.

Adapted from *Smart Girls, Gifted Women,* by Barbara Kerr (Columbus, OH: Ohio Psychology Publishing Company, 1985. Reprinted by permission of the publisher.

The most vulnerable stage for gifted girls — the time when juggling friends, school, and family seems like a never-ending struggle — often comes during junior high. Puberty sets in, and suddenly the feelings of comfort and security experienced during childhood are replaced by insecurity and emotional turbulence.

A teacher we know interviewed a group of gifted females to find out what they were thinking and feeling. At the time of the interview, Helena, Regan, Diana, and Keri were all in junior high; Rhonda was 18 and in her last year of high school. (Thanks to Stephanie Bays, Elyria, Ohio, for allowing us to use this excerpt from her interview project.)

▶ On Expectations

Helena: "My parents ride my brother to get good grades, but they don't do anything to me. They just say 'that's good' and then go talk to my brother."

Regan: "If I get A's and B's, it's a good job. But my brother gets congratulated all over if he gets an A. **He** gets a celebration."

Rhonda: "It gets old after a while, especially after you get into high school. You just don't want to bother anymore."

▶ On Popularity

Rhonda: "Guys don't like girls who are smarter than they are."

Regan: "Most probably they think that you're a brain and all you do is study."

Diana: "But most of the popular girls — the cheerleader types — are really smart."

Teacher: "Do you think they're popular because they're cheerleaders, or because they're gifted?"

All: "Cheerleaders!"

Rhonda: "When I was in junior high the guys didn't like the competition from the girls. If you were smart, you were —"

Regan: "You were outlawed."

Rhonda: "You weren't a girl, you were a brain."

"Now, we are becoming the men we wanted to marry. Once women were trained to marry a doctor, not be one."
— *Gloria Steinem*

▶ **On Careers**

Keri: "I want to get something more out of life than being tied down to a bunch of kids. I'm going to start my career in medicine first and then maybe get married."

Regan: "It would be boring if my husband went out and made the money, then came home and griped about it."

Rhonda: "For me, a career is not so much the money. I'd like to be able to look back and not have any regrets about not doing what I wanted to do. I'd want the money, I'd like the money, but at the same time I want to be happy myself. Also, I think I have to be happy with myself before I can make anyone else happy in a relationship."

Teacher: "You're talking about self-fulfillment."

Rhonda: "Yes. And as I get older, it gets easier. It's not so much 'you're gifted, so you have to do this and that,' it's more of a sense of security, a belief that you can make it on your own. You *have* the ability, and as long as you're comfortable with yourself, it doesn't really matter what other people think or say."

Gifted girls, gifted boys: both deserve to know that they are valuable and capable. To dismiss a person's achievements because "you're *only* a girl" is as ignorant and shortsighted as saying, "I expect you to do well *because* you're a boy."

Every sexual stereotype has two sides. If girls are "supposed to be" loving and affectionate with children, then boys "should be" less so. If girls are "supposed to be" emotional, then boys "shouldn't" cry. If girls are "supposed to be" housewives, then boys "had better" grow up expecting to become the family breadwinners. See how each stereotype robs everyone of their individual freedoms?

It's simply not fair to be judged on the basis of something you can't control — your sex. We can all profit by letting go of the idea that genius or gentleness is determined by gender.

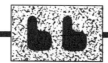

"Don't shut yourself up in a bandbox because you are a woman, but understand what is going on, and educate yourself to take part in the world's work for it all affects you and yours."
— *Louisa May Alcott*

GROWING PAINS

We all have favorite teachers — ones who made a difference in our lives, who inspired us, or brought out the best in us, or taught us something that changed us forever. For Jim, that teacher was a man named Mr. Maloney. Jim tells why he will never forget him:

"I was in Mr. Maloney's American Government class in the fall of 1971, a time when the Vietnam War still made daily headlines and 'body count' was part of our everyday vocabulary. On many occasions our class discussions drifted away from an analysis of the Constitution into other issues more closely related to our own minds and times. We talked about Saigon, the POWs, draft resistance, and our friends and relatives whose brothers, sons, sisters, or fathers had lost their lives in that parabolic curve of Southeast Asia. Back then it seemed that everyone knew someone whose life ended while fighting that never-declared 'war'. . . .

"In Mr. Maloney's class, we aired our anger, our grief, and sometimes the fear that we, too, would soon be drafted into service. On some days our questions were probably naive, but even the most innocent among us held personal opinions — everyone, that is, except Keith.

"Keith dismissed our discussions as 'fruitless' and 'off the topic.' An intelligent person who planned on going to college after graduation, he saw no reason to talk about present-day events. To him, history was what had already occurred, not what was happening today.

"Intimidated at times by Keith's criticism, Mr. Maloney would often steer us back to the subject at hand. But one day he laid into him.

"'Keith,' he said, 'you might not want to hear about Vietnam, but avoiding it is not going to make it go away.'

"A lot has happened since 1971. Both Keith and I graduated from high school and went on to college and beyond. Vietnam gradually faded from our everyday awareness, although many people still bear the emotional and physical scars. Mr. Maloney retired last year; Saigon has become Ho Chi Minh City.

"I've forgotten many of the facts, dates, and ideas that American Government class was supposed to burn into my brain. But one thing I never forgot (and probably never will) was what Mr. Maloney told Keith that day. I learned from him that even though the 'real world' can hurt, it won't go away. Avoiding unpleasant topics can't make them disappear."

What's the point behind this parable? To underscore the truth that there are times and events that happen to us, to people we care about, and to our planet that bother us deeply. From world hunger to the potential for nuclear war, from last night's fight with your parents to the zit on your forehead, we all have concerns that shake our complacency and give us pause. Whether a problem is minute or massive, personal or international in scope, it can be accompanied by perceptible anxiety, pain, and fear.

How can we learn to deal with those feelings? How can we keep them from getting us down? How can we make it through the rough times and equip ourselves to cope with those to come?

Good questions. Now let's consider some possible answers.

COUNTERING THE "YOU'RE-JUST-A-KID" SYNDROME

 When a group of gifted teenagers from New York was polled about questions they have about themselves and the world, they came up with the following:

▶ "Does God really exist?"

▶ "What will it feel like to die?"

▶ "Is there someone (ANYONE?) who thinks and looks at life the way I do?"

▶ "Are scientific experiments in the search for truth always justifiable?"

▶ "Will the universe ever come to an end?"

Some of these questions have many answers, depending on individual philosophies, beliefs, experiences, and so on. Others seem more rhetorical — the kinds of questions that pit you against Aristotle, Gandhi, or your parents when *your* sense of truth differs from *theirs*. Thus, the hardest part of answering the above questions (and others like them) often comes in trying to justify to others *why* you believe *what* you believe.

As John Lennon once explained:

> "There was something wrong with me, I thought, because I seemed to see things other people didn't see. I thought I was crazy or an egomaniac for claiming to see things other people didn't see. As a child I would say, 'But this is going on!' and everybody would look at me as if I was crazy."

From "The Me I See: Self-Images of the Gifted Child," *Teaching Gifted Children*, July/August 1981, p. 9.

When you see black when everyone else sees white or when you see shades of gray that no one else seems able to perceive, you may start to feel lonely, afraid, or different. Well-meaning others may try to convince you that your perceptions will change as you mature, or they may try to persuade you to ignore your own ideas in deference to theirs.

What can you do when someone puts you off, puts you down, or offers to do your thinking for you? Here are suggestions that have worked for teenagers we know. They might work for you, too.

Respect Yourself

Have you ever asked an adult a question and been told, "Don't worry about that — you're just a kid"? Usually, this response comes from someone who thinks you're too young to be thinking "such things." ("Such things" usually translates into questions about sex, religion, politics, or other so-called adult topics.)

"The real questions are the ones that obtrude upon your consciousness whether you like it or not, the ones that make your mind start vibrating like a jackhammer, the ones that you 'come to terms with' only to discover that they are still there. The real questions refuse to be placated."
— *Ingrid Bengis*

The fact is, you can't *not* think about ideas that enter your mind at an earlier age than they're "supposed to." It's like telling a bumblebee that it's not supposed to fly. Interestingly, there's a scientific theory that says just that. According to the Theory of Uneven Weight, the bumblebee is too top-heavy to support itself in flight. Yet the bumblebee flies anyway because it doesn't know how *not* to.

"Poor guy — he just fell for the Theory of Uneven Weight."

Perhaps the tendency to ask big questions and think big thoughts early in life is part of what being gifted is all about. And even though it may make some social interactions more difficult than you'd like them to be, you're going to have to live with it — because that's the way it is.

Don't give in to people who tell you to turn off your brain. Your cranium is private property, and what goes on up there is up to you. Respect your abilities — and *respect yourself*.

It may help to know that when others try to put you on intellectual hold, it may be an instinctive reaction against an idea *they* don't understand. And when they won't answer your questions, it may be because they can't.

So, where can you go for answers? The library, for starters (obviously!). Read what other great thinkers have thought and written and said. (They won't always agree, which will give you even more to think about.) Find out the facts on issues that concern you. Then

WHAT'S YOUR OPINION?

Every year since 1969, America's top-achieving teenagers have been asked their opinions of certain timely issues. In the 1986 *17th Annual Survey of High Achievers*, published by "Who's Who Among American High School Students," 5,000 students gave their opinions on a variety of subjects. Here are a few of the results of the survey:

▶ *On "taboo topics":*

— 63% do not believe that sex is an expected part of a teenage relationship.

— 81% report never having used marijuana, cocaine, or other drugs (excluding alcohol).

— 46% state that they know someone who has committed or attempted suicide.

— When asked to give the reasons for teen suicide, 86% said feelings of personal worthlessness, 81% said feelings of isolation and loneliness, and 72% said the pressure to achieve.

▶ *On politics:*

— If asked to vote for a president today, 49% would vote Republican, 25% Democrat, and 16% independent.

— 39% believe that the U.S. government's top domestic priority should be improving education.

— 83% favor an arms limitation agreement between the United States and the Soviet Union.

— 57% believe that nuclear arms use and production should be banned totally.

▶ *On teachers:*

— 73% believe that if teachers were evaluated periodically, student achievement would rise.

— 64% believe that more difficult qualification standards should be used when selecting teachers or school administrators.

find out where to go to learn more, and more, and more; research can be a long and fascinating path.

Get involved with people who have concerns similar to yours. Worried about the environment? Consider joining the Sierra Club or Greenpeace. Worried about the Bomb? Become a member of STOP. There are all sorts of organizations you can explore. Start with these:

SIERRA CLUB
PO Box 7959
San Francisco, CA 94120-9943

GREENPEACE
1611 Connecticut Ave., N.W.
PO Box 3720
Washington, D.C. 20007

NATIONAL WILDLIFE FEDERATION
1412 Sixteenth St., N.W.
Washington, D.C. 20036-2266

PEOPLE FOR THE ETHICAL TREATMENT OF ANIMALS
PO Box 42516
Washington, D.C. 20015

STOP (Students and Teachers Organization to Prevent
Nuclear War)
636 Beacon St., Room 203
Boston, MA 02215

WORLD FUTURE SOCIETY
4916 St. Elmo Ave.
Bethesda, MD 20814

NATIONAL ORGANIZATION FOR WOMEN
1401 New York Ave., N.W.
Washington, D.C. 20005

UNICEF (United Nations Children's Fund)
866 United Nations Plaza
New York, NY 10001

Find adults you can talk to; they're out there. Your parents may welcome the opportunity to have "serious conversations" with you. So may a teacher or two (or more). Take your questions about religion to a pastor, priest, or rabbi — or all three. Use a class project or an assignment for the school paper as a chance to interview politicians, scientists, university professors, health professionals, whoever.

Don't give up! If *you* think a question is important enough to pursue, IT IS.

"It is better to know some of the questions than all of the answers."
— *James Thurber*

Learn to Suffer Fools Gladly

Did you ever go to see a movie you *knew* would be awful, just because your friends wanted to see it? Have you ever come up with an answer in class and kept it to yourself, waiting for other students to arrive at the same solution? Have you ever resisted the urge to point out a teacher's mistake or to argue with your parents when you're *positive* you're right?

If you've done any of the above, without thinking too hard about it or passing negative judgments on the other people involved, then you have probably learned how, why, when, and where to **Suffer Fools Gladly** (SFG).

SFG. It's a codeword, a survival technique, a social grace. Its earliest known mention is in the Bible, 2 Corinthians 11:19: "For ye suffer fools gladly, seeing ye *yourselves* are wise." What it implies to us is that there are times when it's best — even smartest — to go along with the crowd, rather than assert your rights as an individual.

Mastering the art of SFG doesn't mean you're a bad person, a phony, or two-faced. On the contrary, it shows that you know how to play the game of life by some unwritten but well-understood rules of group consensus.

Why *not* go to the movie? It may not have won first prize at Cannes, but that doesn't mean you can't have fun watching it with your friends. Why *not* give others in your class the chance to speak up and shine? They have that right as surely as you do — and who knows, you may learn something from them. Why *not* keep silent about a teacher's blunder? If you must talk about it, arrange to meet privately after class. Why *not* go along with your parents for a change? Maybe they know something you don't. Or maybe the point simply isn't important enough to argue about.

Think of the times when others have suffered you. (Just because you're smart doesn't mean your ideas are *always* the best or the brightest.) Your parents have probably put up with all kinds of nonsense from you over the years. Your teachers have probably been patient on a number of occasions when you've gone off on tangents. And your friends have stuck by you in spite of your quirks and flaws.

Naturally, it's important to know when *not* to SFG: when your safety is at stake, when "the crowd" puts others in danger or humiliates or hurts them, or when your values, morals, beliefs, or integrity are at risk of being compromised. When in doubt, ask yourself this question: "If I go along with this, will it make any difference a year from now?" If the answer is "no," then swallow hard, smile, and try to enjoy yourself. If the answer is "yes" or "maybe," then swallow hard, say "no thanks," and pat yourself on the back for making a tough and not too popular decision.

"If everyone else wants to see Ninja Neighbors *instead* of Casablanca, I guess I can go along with that."

Find Other People Who Like You the Way You Are

One teacher of gifted kids observed, "My exposure to gifted students has made me fully aware that we are not all equal. . . .Some 10-year-olds are as comfortable with $E = MC^2$ as they are with balloons, books, and baseball."

For a 10-year-old whose mind grasps the theory of relativity or the 15-year-old whose goal is to discover a cure for cancer, friendship — *true* friendship that involves sharing, understanding, and mutual respect — may seem rare or even unattainable. As a last resort, some gifted students often seek relationships either with adults or with kids who are a few years older than they are. (Like water, the intellect seeks its own level.)

There's nothing wrong with that! As an adult, you'll have friends, colleagues, and co-workers who are old enough to be your grandparents or young enough to be your children. About the only time in life when friendships are pigeonholed by age is from kindergarten to grade 12. After that, age matters less and other things matter more — like compatibility, common interests, and the countless other factors that bring people together.

As one woman in her 30s says, "My friends run the gamut when it comes to age — from their early 20s all the way up to 60. One is 15 years younger than I am, and another is older than my mom. I was in college before I discovered the difference between 'agemate' and 'peer,' and I wish I'd figured it out a lot sooner."

How can you meet people who are likely to be your peers? It's tough to do this at school, where grade levels still function as social barriers. It may be easier if you're in an open or nontraditional school, where students from different grades are grouped in homerooms and take classes together. (Actually, this isn't such a modern notion after all; it happened in the one-room schools our grandparents and great-grandparents went to.)

You may have better luck if you look outside school for opportunities to meet and make friends. For example:

- Take a class through a university extension or adult education program, which attract people of all ages. Or see what's available at your local community college or neighborhood recreation center.
- If your interests lie in the arts, volunteer to work at a museum or usher at a concert hall or theater. Find out about special projects or activities that use volunteers, and then get involved. (At the Science Museum of Minnesota, groups gather on the weekends to build dinosaurs from bones discovered in digs.)
- Join a hobby club or other special-interest group. If you're into computers, try a local users' group. If you play a musical instrument, look into a community orchestra or band. (Or start a small ensemble of your own.) If you're passionate about science fiction, mystery novels, or Victorian poetry, check out a book discussion group.

TEN TIPS FOR MAKING AND KEEPING FRIENDS

1. Reach out; don't always wait for someone else to make the first move. A simple "hi" and a smile go a long way.

2. Let people know that you're interested in them. Don't just talk about yourself; ask questions about *others*. (Once you've mastered this, you'll have the art of conversation down pat. It's amazing how many people are incompetent at this basic social skill.)

3. Be a good listener. This means looking at people while they're talking to you and genuinely paying attention to what they're saying. (A long litany of "uh-huhs" is a dead giveaway that your mind is somewhere else.)

4. Don't be a show-off. Not everyone you meet will have your abilities and interests, but that doesn't mean you have to rub it in. (On the other hand, you shouldn't have to hide your abilities — which you won't, once you find people who like you the way you are.)

5. Be honest. Tell the truth about yourself and your convictions. When asked for your opinion, be sincere. Friends appreciate forthrightness in each other. BUT . . .

6. When necessary, temper your honesty with diplomacy. The truth doesn't have to hurt. It's better to say "Gee, your new haircut is interesting" rather than "You actually paid money for THAT?" There are times when frankness is inappropriate and unnecessary.

7. Don't just use your friends as sounding boards for your problems and complaints. Include them in the good times, too.

8. Do your share of the work. That's right, *work.* Any relationship takes effort. Don't always depend on your friends to make all the plans and carry all the weight.

9. Be accepting. Not all of your friends have to think and act like you do. (Wouldn't it be boring if they did?)

10. Learn to recognize the so-called friends you can do without. Some gifted kids get so lonely that they put up with anyone — including friends who aren't really friends at all. Follow tips 1–9 and and this shouldn't happen to you!

FRIENDSHIP VS. POPULARITY

There's a big difference between having friends and being popular. It may be hard to recognize at times when you seem to be the only person *not* surrounded by a crowd of admirers and acquaintances. But the distinction is a real and important one. As one Canadian college student explained:

> "It is only in the last year and a half that I've discovered the delights of belonging in a group of real friends. We are an odd, sometimes ridiculous crew who are accepted as such by others. . . . Many kids who have social problems in high school discover that things get better by the second or third year of university — maybe earlier, depending on how quickly they learn the rules.
>
> "It's no fun to go through bad social times, but I know now that I wouldn't trade popularity and 'ordinariness' for the solid friendships and ability to function on my own that I have now."

A wise old grown-up in her 30s looks back at her high-school years and remembers:

> "It wasn't until my senior year that I 'fell into' a group of friends. Up until then, I'd been a real loner. I was the 'class brain,' the one with the glasses and funny hair and weird clothes who never fit in, never went out, never got asked on dates. Then my English teacher pushed me to join the

newspaper staff, and guess what? Everyone there was brainy, wore glasses, and had funny hair and unfashionable clothes. Even better, they all went out together, and suddenly I was included in group parties and picnics and social events. None of us was popular in school — but we were all popular with each other. Each of us was a social misfit outside the newspaper office, but inside, we were IT!"

Things *will* get better if you're willing to be patient and make the effort. These Survival Tips, gleaned from the experience of people who have been there, should help:

▶ Be content with one or two solid friendships; they're worth more than you realize. Don't expect *everyone* to like you. (Do **you** like everyone you meet?)

▶ Seek out activities and groups that form around a common interest (photography clubs, surfing freaks, foreign language nuts). Don't let your relationships be determined by age alone.

▶ Talk to your parents — sometimes to get advice and sometimes just to sound off. Problems tend to get less complicated if you share them.

▶ Be yourself. It's too tiring to maintain a facade for someone else's sake; besides, you're bound to be found out sooner or later. Friendships work best when they're aboveboard.

SOME FINE-LINE DISTINCTIONS

The difference between . . . is that . . .

Friendship and popularity

Friendship implies acceptance of you at all times, while **popularity** means that you're accepted only when it's convenient or chic.

Loneliness and being alone

Loneliness hurts, while **being alone** feels good because it gives you the chance to experience solitude and freedom.

Giving in and giving up

Giving in means that you trust others enough to respect their judgments, while **giving up** implies a sense of despair, resignation, and an inner feeling that "my ideas are lousy."

Age and maturity

Age is a number that happens to you, while **maturity** is an attitude and a set of behaviors you develop to face facts, set goals, and dream dreams.

Knowledge and wisdom

Knowledge is a storehouse of facts, while **wisdom** is the ability to take your knowledge and use it to improve your life and the lives of others.

UNDERSTANDING ADOLESCENCE (OR TRYING TO)

One reason that it's tough being a teenager is that you have to be an adolescent at the same time. It would be nice to be able to postpone adolescence until you were ready for it, but that's simply not possible.

Actually, adolescence is a 20th century invention. In the 1800s, a person went directly from childhood to adult responsibilities like work and family. A mere three generations later, a person might spend the years between 13 and 24 going to high school, then college, then graduate school without dipping a toe into the real world. There's no social track record for what's supposed to happen during this long and tumultuous period.

Why do some people sail through adolescence seemingly effortlessly, while others fall apart at the first hint of hormones? Why do some have good looks and energy to spare, while others lurch around like Quasimodo in a semicoma? Why do some later think back on their teenage years as "the best in their lives," while others compare theirs to an extended stay in Motel Hell?

Experts who study adolescents have discovered some similarities among this group of very different individuals. The most obvious are the physical changes that pave the road from childhood to young adulthood. Who doesn't know about growth spurts, cracking voices, pimples, the sudden compelling and confusing interest in sex, and the myriad other burdens of puberty? These combine to

121

create the feeling of being out of control and overwhelmed by strange and powerful forces from within. Add to this the expectations the world lays on you just because you're growing up, and it's no wonder teenagers get cranky.

Then there are the social and emotional issues. On the one hand, you're learning that you're different from everyone else, an individual, unique. On the other, you're finding out fast how important it is to fit into society and the world. Just as you're starting to figure out your family, you're preparing to leave it and go off on your own. One day, you're getting your act together, and the next, you're taking it on the road.

Thomas M. Buescher, associate director of the Midwest Talent Search Project and faculty member at Northwestern University, has identified six issues of special relevance to gifted adolescents. They are:

1. Ownership: *"Who says I'm gifted?"*

In junior and senior high school, being popular usually means being normal or familiar. Popular leaders represent the more dominant values of the group; popular girls look and dress according to group tastes; popular guys use language adopted by the dominant clique. In other words, popularity depends on conformity — something gifted students often aren't very good at.

It may seem better to deny your ability in order to appear normal and fit in. And it may be easy to do this — for a while. The eventual result is internal conflict. Resolving it means going back to owning who you are, what you are, and what you're capable of. The only *real* answer to "Who says I'm gifted?" is "*I* do!"

2. Dissonance: *"If I'm so smart, why can't I do everything right?"*

Prone to perfectionism from an early age, gifted kids have an especially hard time during adolescence. Already off-balance because of all the physical, social, and emotional changes going on, they feel a real dissonance between how well *they do* and how well *they think* they should do.

Your talents and abilities are growing, but even you have limitations! Becoming aware of them and learning to live with them doesn't mean you're giving up; instead, it means you're *growing* up.

3. Risk Taking: *"Should I, or shouldn't I?"*

One of the characteristics of the young gifted child is the willingness to take risks. Gifted adolescents, on the other hand, seem to become *more* cautious while their normal friends become *less* cautious by the minute.

No one seems quite sure why this happens. Maybe it's because gifted teenagers are more aware of the consequences of risky actions and more skilled at checking out the advantages and disadvantages ahead of time. In any case, they seem to need security — and may scale back their activities to get it.

Are you avoiding honors courses because you can't be sure of getting A's? Are you choosing not to challenge yourself because you can't predict the outcome? There's such a thing as being *too* careful. Remember the old saying: Nothing ventured, nothing gained.

4. Others' Expectations: *"Who's in charge here?"*

You have goals for yourself. Your parents, teachers, friends, and relatives have goals for you, too, and they're probably not shy about making them known. What happens when their push meets with your pull? A competition of Olympic proportions that can leave you feeling frustrated, resentful, and confused.

Multipotential makes this especially difficult. The more you *can* do, the more you (and others) think you *should* do, and the more people around you try to guide you "for your own good."

What's the solution? Until you're on your own, you'll have to put up with some outside interference. Just remember that in the final analysis, it *is* your life, and you're the only one who can live it.

5. Impatience: *"I want it NOW!"*

Gifted teenagers don't hold the patent on impatience, a universal adolescent trait. They can, however, carry it too far. They tend to want clear-cut answers to *everything* — complex problems, career choices, even personal relationships.

Sometimes those clear-cut answers don't exist. Sometimes they take a long time to make themselves known. Impatience can lead to hasty resolutions that leave you feeling angry and disappointed.

This doesn't mean that you should spend hours agonizing over which socks to wear. But when it comes to the Big Issues — like what to be when you grow up or how to resolve a difference with a friend — it makes sense to go slow.

6. Identity: *"I know who I am and what I want to be!"*

Competing expectations and impatience can propel gifted adolescents toward deciding their futures too soon. The 14-year-old who declares he's premed is closing the door to other opportunities. And the 16-year-old who plans for a career in dance may never discover her talents in math or science.

One man in his late 20s recalls an argument he had with his father at age 13:

> "I had decided that I wanted to be an English teacher. My dad wanted me to take more science courses. I told him that those didn't have anything to do with teaching English. 'Take them anyway,' he suggested. 'Why narrow your options?' 'I know what I want to be,' I shouted, 'and I'LL NEVER CHANGE!' Today I remember that as one of the dumbest things I ever said."

Narrowing your interests early can prevent you from reaching your full potential. It can keep you from the satisfying, integrated careers and relationships that make the most of your abilities. Besides, whoever said you have to decide *now* what you'll be for the rest of your life?

It's okay to stay a kid for a few more years. One of the bonuses of adolescence is that it buys you time to experiment, explore, and experience a variety of possibilities and choices.

Many employers today acknowledge that early specialization may not be the way to go. Instead of hiring M.B.A.s, they're looking for liberal arts graduates — a shift that implies an important message.

Adapted from "A Framework for Understanding the Social and Emotional Development of Gifted and Talented Adolescents," by Thomas M. Buescher, *Roeper Review*, Vol. 8, No. 1, September 1985, pp. 12–15. Reprinted with permission.

"I think what is happening to me is so wonderful, and not only what can be seen on my body, but all that is taking place inside. I never discuss myself or any of these things with anybody; that is why I have to talk to myself about them."
— Anne Frank, The Diary of a Young Girl

To find out more about the phenomenon called *adolescence*, read:

The Teenage Survival Book, by Sol Gordon (New York: Times Books, 1981).

Bringing Up Parents, by Alex J. Packer (Washington, D.C.: Acropolis Books, 1985).

DEATH WITH HONORS: SUICIDE AMONG GIFTED ADOLESCENTS

T here are a few topics that are so taboo and painful to discuss that many people choose to ignore them entirely. Teenage suicide is one of them. Working under the misguided assumption that "If you don't talk about suicide, it will go away" (or "If you do talk about it, more suicides will occur"), many teens and adults dismiss it as something that happens to *other* families in *other* towns. And a lot of people believe that gifted adolescents are too smart to even consider ending their own lives.

Katy Amundson* was 17 when she killed herself. She was an A student and a regular member of her school's Honor Society for academic achievement. She was also a cheerleader, a model, a beauty contestant, and a driven perfectionist who battled both anorexia and bulimia. One February afternoon, she drove to a state park, poured two cans of gasoline over herself, and lit a match.

Teenage suicide is a far bigger problem than most people think. Here are some scary facts:

▶ 6,000 teenagers take their own lives each year. That's about 16 each day — half the size of your homeroom class (or more).

▶ For every suicide, there are at least ten attempts by teenagers to end their lives. That's 60,000 attempts each year — more

* Her name has been changed, but the story is true.

than the total population of Beverly Hills, California; Council Bluffs, Iowa; or Sarasota, Florida.

▶ In a recent poll of 5,000 teenagers listed in *Who's Who Among American High School Students*, 31% said they had considered suicide.

Who is the typical candidate for teenage suicide? Here's a composite picture: male or female, smart or average, a social isolate or a social mixer, from a broken home or a secure one, wealthy or poor, religious or not, black or white, from a suburb or a small town. In other words, there is **no such thing** as a typical suicidal teen. There do appear to be some patterns or trends, but many suicide victims do not fit any particular mold.

• Like Katy Amundson.

• And Keith, who hanged himself in a public restroom. This handsome, intelligent teen from a New England state was a football team captain who, according to his father, "still kissed me goodnight even though he was 16."

• And Melissa and Mary, two 15-year-olds who wrote suicide notes asking their parents for forgiveness. "I love you all, so please don't be sad," wrote Mary. "It's not your fault for having the gun around."

• And Steven, a blonde, blue-eyed 13-year-old who shot himself in the head during reading class. Steven was an A student who had been identified as gifted. He was also a star player on his school basketball team.

Sadly, the list goes on. We could fill this book with stories as tragic as these.

Giftedness and Suicide: Some Possible Explanations

Although there is no firm evidence that gifted teenagers are more likely to attempt/commit suicide than less able adolescents, some aspects of being gifted may in some cases contribute to suicidal behavior. (We have deliberately qualified this statement with "may" and "in some cases" because it is simply *not true* that being gifted makes one more prone to suicide.)

For example:

▶ A perception of failure that differs from *others'* perceptions of failure. (For example, feeling that a B is equivalent to an F if your personal standard of success calls for an A or above.)

▶ External pressures to always be #1 and a life orientation that identifies one as a "future leader" or a "mover and shaker of the next generation."

▶ The frustration that comes when one's intellectual talents outpace his or her social or physical development. ("For being so smart, I'm awfully dumb at making friends" or "Starting school early and skipping second grade was fine, but now I'm the freak of the locker room — I'm so puny!")

▶ The ability to understand adult situations and world events while being powerless to effect any change. (After all, "you're just a kid.")

These problems don't plague all (or even most) gifted teenagers, and you may not identify with any of them. If so, that's fine; you can ignore the next few pages. But if any of these things do concern you, read on.

Knowing and Accepting Yourself

If you take a moment to consider how people behave differently in similar circumstances, the complexity of the human animal becomes clear. Some people seem so sensitive to criticism that an unfriendly glance causes shame and tears. Others would interpret a brick thrown through their windshield simply as an odd way of saying hello.

It's the same with issues related to growing up. What one teenager may view as a catastrophe, another may perceive as an opportunity. And it's the same with issues as heavy as suicide. Herman Hesse put it this way:

> "Just as there are those who at the least indisposition develop a fever, so do those whom we call suicides, and who are always very emotional and sensitive, develop at the least shock the notion of suicide. Had we a science with the courage and authority to concern itself with mankind . . . these matters of fact would be familiar to everyone."

From *Steppenwolf* (New York: Bantam Books, 1974), p. 55.

The science of understanding human behavior is a soft science at best. There are no guarantees that people will always respond in the same way to the same situation. This is what makes human psychology so fascinating (and so frustrating).

Psychologists and educators do seem to agree that there are two keys to coping with bad times: *understanding yourself* and *developing and maintaining a positive attitude toward yourself and others*. They have come up with some suggestions, based on research studies and life experiences, for directing people toward a healthy outlook on life.

1. Read about who you are and others like you who have gone before.

Psychologists call this *identification*. What it means is that you should try to find another person — a historical figure or the guy next door — who shares some of your goals, attitudes, fears, and beliefs.

Books like *The Courage of Conviction* will show you that many successful people — Billy Graham, Lech Walesa, Jane Alexander, Joan Baez, and Mario Cuomo, to name a few — have developed a philosophy of life that allows for human frailties and fears.

For example, here's Steve Allen describing why there is no "one right answer" that applies to every life situation:

> "No philosophy, sadly, has all the answers. No matter how assured we may be about certain aspects of our belief, there are always painful inconsistencies, exceptions and contradictions. This is as true in religion as it is in politics, and is self-evident to all except fanatics and the naive."

From *The Courage of Conviction*, Philip L. Berman, ed. (New York: Dodd, Mead and Company, 1985), p. 9.

2. Try to remember that life isn't always fair, winning isn't always best, and many questions don't have "one right answer."

Our society does a lot to encourage and reward achievement — which is okay to a point, because winning is nothing to be ashamed of. Still, there seems to be the prevailing attitude that the *only* measure of success is achievement. This discredits a lot of very good ideas (and the people behind them) that never achieve #1 status.

For example, after four years of high school, only one person is chosen to be valedictorian, which leaves many "also rans" wondering, "What's the point?"

The point is that life isn't fair. This may be a cliché, but it's true anyway. So is the old saw that says, "It's not whether you win or lose but how you play the game." There's comfort to be derived from platitudes like these.

Do your best not to get too upset when your burning questions about God, the meaning of life, and the pursuit of happiness don't get answered immediately or to your full satisfaction. Life is a journey, not a destination, so answers that seem solid now may seem silly in two years. And questions that mean nothing to you today may represent great challenges later.

3. Cultivate and maintain a healthy skepticism.

Henry James, the 19th century author of *A Turn of the Screw*, once wrote: "Steer safely between the opposite dangers of believing too little or believing too much." More recently, a popular bumper sticker has put this more succinctly: "Question Authority."

Sometimes the right path for you may not be the most popular one. Being gifted, you have the ability to detect nuances that aren't obvious to other people. You can draw connections between ideas that seem totally unrelated to those around you. If you choose to act on your convictions, you may indeed find yourself in a minority of one.

As a gifted 21-year-old observed, "True genius requires creativity along with (or perhaps in spite of) intelligence. The invention of new ideas . . . can be painful, lonely, and difficult."

132

THE SEVEN GREAT MYTHS OF ADOLESCENCE: ROADBLOCKS TO SELF-APPRECIATION

1. *Everyone has to like me.*

2. *I have to like everyone.*

3. *Happiness is achieved solely through wealth or power.*

4. *No one will find me physically attractive enough to want to date me.*

5. *Asking for help from parents, teachers, friends, and others is the same as admitting failure.*

6. *There's nothing left to learn and no one around who can teach me anything.*

7. *If I can't do something perfectly, I shouldn't do it at all.*

Don't put yourself down by minimizing your powerhouse ideas —
if, in fact, you believe in them and in yourself. You may not find anyone who agrees with you, but you'll be in impressive historical company. Many of the world's great thinkers have stood alone in their
attitudes and philosophies.

What does all of this have to do with teenage suicide?   Plenty. Nobody really wants to die; instead, there are people who don't want
to live. There's a *big* difference. The circumstances that prompt suicidal gestures are the everyday frustrations that people feel alone
in facing or impotent to overcome.

Although it may not seem true at times, we all share a common
bond called *humanity*. To feel the way it holds us close, we must
take a few moments now and then for deep personal reflection.

▼▼▼

**To find out more about ways to know and accept yourself,
read:**

Why Am I Afraid to Tell You Who I Am? by John Powell (Illinois: Ar-
gus Communications, 1969).

*The Courage of Conviction: Prominent Contemporaries Discuss
Their Beliefs and How They Put Them Into Action,* edited by Philip
L. Berman (New York: Dodd, Mead and Company, 1985).

▲▲▲

Intervening with a Friend in Need

According to data from the health professions, the incidences of
depression now outnumber those of all other medical symptoms put
together. Blame it on world strife, the loss of traditional family values, or the sense of personal isolation that results from living in
complex and uncompromising times. Whatever the reason, the reality is that a lot of young people see more bad than good. They wonder if life is all it's cracked up to be. They fail to see alternatives to
living the way they do. **They need help.**

Not everyone is a counselor, and not every teenager is equipped to offer the long-term treatment a depressed friend may require to weather emotionally troubling times. But most can listen, and sometimes, that's enough.

Depression is an illness. A depressed person can't fight it by himself or herself, any more than you can fight strep throat with cough drops. Often, depression requires medical attention. Most of the time, however, depressed adolescents will go first to agemates, not to adults, to discuss what's bothering them. That's where you come in, ears wide open and shoulder ready for a cry.

There are a number of ways you can help a friend in need. To make them easier to remember, we've organized them around the acronym **REALITY.**

Respect

Respect your friend's self-doubts and sadness. Don't dismiss his feelings or beliefs as being silly or trivial. Share some of your own fears and losses. Let him know that you appreciate his willingness to open up to you; this implies trust, and it takes courage to admit "I hurt."

Evaluate

Evaluate your friend's words and ask, "So how can I help?" or "How do you plan to deal with these problems?" If she even intimates that suicide is a possibility, keep her talking! The more specific her plans are, the more imminent the danger is.

Act

Act specifically. Too often, teenagers feel that they can't share with others (especially adults) things that were said to them in confidence. While this applies in many cases, it *never* applies to life-threatening situations. Let your friend know that while you'd never do anything to hurt him, you *will* do whatever you can to keep him alive. Then talk to an adult — a sympathetic teacher, a school counselor, someone in your church or synagogue, anyone who can help you intervene.

A suicide claims more than one victim. It leaves behind a host of people who carry the burden of believing that they could and should have done something to stop it. Don't put yourself behind this emotional eightball.

Listen

The most difficult of all human relations skills, *true listening* involves understanding the other person's words *and intentions*. It doesn't mean waiting for your turn to talk, nor does it lead to a verbal battle of "I'm right/You're wrong." As one suicidal teenager wrote, "I didn't expect anyone to give me all the answers. I only wanted someone to hear my questions."

Investigate

Investigate local agencies. Know where to go for more help than you can give. Find out where teenagers in your community can get confidential information and advice about problems they're unwilling to discuss with someone at home or school. Start by checking your local Yellow Pages under "Crisis Intervention Centers." (Additional resources are listed at the end of this section.)

Take

Take preventive steps. Plano, Texas, a town that grew from 3,000 to 93,000 people in just ten years, had big problems with teenage suicide, delinquency, and drug abuse. In response, a task force of teenagers, teachers, and community leaders began to meet regularly with newcomers and anyone else who wanted to talk or listen. The result? No teenage suicides in over a year.

Talk to school or church leaders about starting a peer support group to serve as a forum for discussing the problems (and joys) of growing up. These meetings can perform much the same function as an annual medical checkup or car tuneup: detecting potential problems.

Yourself

Just because we don't have degrees in counseling, we assume that we can't help a friend in need, pain, or crisis. Wrong! Each of us *can* help simply by serving as the initial contact person. We can listen, ask questions, smile, and reach out a comforting hand. Simply by being supportive, we can bolster a friend's feelings of self-worth. We can make a difference.

"The way in which my own life touches those of so many others, those I know and thousands of those I don't, has strengthened my belief that each human has his or her unique place in the ocean of existence."
— *Jane Goodall*

SUICIDE PREVENTION RESOURCES

If you need more information about suicide or suicide prevention, contact any of the following:

▶ Look under *"Suicide Prevention"* in your local phone book. Most cities and many towns have suicide prevention hotlines staffed 24 hours a day, 7 days a week, with people ready and willing to listen.

▶ *"Metro-Help"* is a toll-free, 24-hours-a-day, 7-days-a-week national crisis hotline for suicidal and runaway youths. Call 1-800-621-4000.

▶ *The National Committee on Youth Suicide Prevention* can provide information and articles on youth suicide and prevention. It has established suicide prevention committees in most states and can refer you to the one nearest you. Call 1-212-677-6666, or write: The National Committee on Youth Suicide Prevention, 67 Irving Place So., New York, NY 10003.

▶ The *Youth Suicide National Center* sends representatives to schools, conducts youth-oriented programs on suicide prevention, provides counseling, and mails out information on suicide. Call 1-202-429-2016, or write: Youth Suicide National Center, 1825 I St. N.W., Suite 400, Washington, D.C. 20006.

GIFTED PEOPLE
SPEAK OUT

Tired of hearing about Einstein, Roosevelt, Beethoven, and other famous late greats? Can't get inspired by those who demonstrated intelligence, creativity, and smarts long before you became part of the gene pool? Want to hear about people who are young, gifted, and talented here, now, and today?

We interviewed one gifted teenager and one postadolescent 25-year-old. Here's what they had to say.

EDWARD

Edward, 25, is working on his Ph.D. in pure mathematics at the University of Wisconsin at Madison.

Tell us about your high school experience.
My high school experience was very good. There were two teachers in particular that I really looked up to. One was my gifted program instructor, and the other was a track coach. They helped me a lot and it was good to have people to emulate and look up to. Just having someone to be there for me and to say, "Hey, what's the worst that can happen?" helped me to take more risks than I might have otherwise.

The gifted class instructor knew that although I was gifted, I was very shy and had a lot of trouble making friends, mostly with girls; getting dates and things like that. He provided me with a lot of support in learning how to be more outgoing and social.

How did you get involved in the gifted program?

My parents initially recommended me for it, and that really surprised me; I guess I never knew they thought that highly of me. I mean, I *know* they thought highly of me, but I thought they felt that way just because I was their son.

A few teachers recommended me for the program, too. We took some kind of IQ test because there had to be test scores to substantiate the recommendations. I did really terrible on the test, just barely above average. When I'd be working on it, I'd find a certain problem very interesting and spend a lot of time on it. I never even finished the test. I don't think those tests mean very much. They don't always measure a variety of intelligences.

How do you feel about the label "gifted"?

I think it can be very negative at times. In high school, it got very bad — in fact, some kids wanted to call the GT program "Godlike Tendencies." There's a lot of stigma attached to it — "so you're gifted, so what can you do?" In classes you were always expected to do well in everything. Some people think you're above them just because you're in the GT program. It can be hard to make friends outside of the program.

I'm definitely an advocate for special programs, but I think they should be called or named for what they do for students or what students can learn in them.

If you had it to do over again, what would you change about high school?

I wish I'd had more exposure to the humanities — music, ballet, dance. I think I spent too much time in the sciences.

What outside activities were you involved in?

Cross-country and track. I also got into burro racing; that's a sport that's only done in Colorado. You run with a burro up to the top of a mountain and then back down. You have to work with the burro all year round, and you really develop a comradeship with your animal. It was a neat thing to do, and I enjoyed it a lot.

I don't run anymore due to a knee injury. But I think the discipline of running really helped me with what I'm doing now. I have to do a lot of studying, mostly on my own, and it's sort of like training for running. It gets lonely at times.

For a long time, running was very important to me. In fact, I had big dreams of being in races like the Western States 100 Mile Run, which is held in the Sierra Nevada mountains. You have to run several 50-mile runs before they'll let you participate, and that's when I came down with my knee injuries. . . . Even after that, I wasn't willing to give up running. Then I injured my ankle and *had* to give it up. I felt like someone had died, because I had nowhere to focus my energies. It took a long time to find out what else I could work on that was challenging. I searched and eventually settled on math.

How was your social life?

At times, I felt like I didn't fit in with others. I still feel that way today. But I've realized that I have access to a lot of ideas and intellectual stimulation that many people can't even dream about. That's consoling for me. I get lonely sometimes, and that makes me realize how I'm different — that I can't just fit in with everyone. It takes me a while to form a close friendship. So sometimes it's hard.

There are a lot of people in my field who are sort of like that, so we can get together and appreciate what we're doing.

How would you describe your learning process?

When I'm learning math, I learn how my brain works, and I find that very fascinating. For example, when I get a homework assignment, I read over all the problems first. Many people will start working on the first one and then continue on in order. But I read all the problems first, even if I can't do them yet. I've found that when I come back to the assignment later, I have ideas on them. By sort of "depositing" the problems in my brain, I start to figure them out even though I'm not actually working on them directly.

I think the subconscious is a very powerful tool in solving problems. I've been practicing visualization lately because I have a Ph.D. qualifying exam coming up. I visualize myself being relaxed and confident during the exam.

I was an engineer as an undergraduate, but that wasn't as challenging as pure mathematics was. So I found my niche in pure mathematics.

What's your favorite goofing-off activity?

I like to do a lot of reading. I read some psychology, and I like to read about how the brain works. I think that if I weren't a mathematician, I'd be a psychologist or a psychiatrist.

I like music. I still like a lot of exercise: biking, walking, volleyball. I'm also quite a baseball fan.

What advice would you give to gifted kids?
I'd like to encourage them to be creative. I get into a mode of playing the necessary games to get a certain grade in a course and just learn the things I need to know for a test. As a result, I sometimes sacrifice my interests and what's out there to learn.

I'd say, be as creative as possible, and explore as many of your interests as possible, even though they might be tangential to what you're supposed to be doing at the time. Or at least store away those interests so you can explore them later.

What advice would you give to teachers and parents of gifted kids?
Don't be intimidated by students who may know more about something than you do or who want to study something you don't know anything about. I think teachers have to have enough self-confidence to say, "Hey, I don't know anything about that, but I can help you find someone who does." Let students explore, and don't look on it as a confrontation.

For that matter, parents don't have to learn everything their kids are interested in, either.

LARA

Lara, 19, is a junior at Macalester College in St. Paul, Minnesota. She skipped 3rd grade and graduated from high school at age 16. Currently, she's a biology major with two minors — one in physics and one in French. She's also working in a lab at 3M doing recombinant DNA research.

Tell us about your high school experience.
I graduated from White Bear Lake Area High School. I was a debater and on the math team. They offered advanced classes for college-bound students. I preferred the language courses; I took five years of French, Spanish, and German. I also enjoyed literature.

I'm very satisfied with my junior and senior high school education. I've talked with kids from all over the country, and I think my high school had a lot to offer. I had to seek it out, though.

White Bear had basically good teachers who were flexible. For example, they allowed me to take two foreign languages at the same time. I'd go to one class one day and the other the next.

I had to ask for things. In fact, I sort of said, "This is what I'm going to do." But they didn't put up too much of a fight. They didn't open any doors for me, but they didn't throw any barriers in my way either.

We had excellent math courses. I got to skip my first year of college calculus because of my training in high school.

What were the characteristics of the teachers you thought were good?
They were flexible . . . . I liked teachers who knew so much that I couldn't comprehend how they could *possibly* know so much. For example, if we were reading a certain book, they would have read three or four books by the same author, plus critiques of their work.

I like teachers who really enjoy teaching and learning new things. I also like teachers who show you how things are related and how they fit with each other.

What were the characteristics of the teachers you didn't like?
There were some teachers who pretended to know a lot and didn't, and they were disappointing. I also didn't like teachers who did a lot of drill and rote work. I like learning in whole pictures, concepts, or ideas rather than a bunch of choppy little facts.

Did you date in high school? How was your social life?
I didn't date. I had a lot of male friends, but I didn't date. My friendships were all platonic, even though people sometimes thought differently. But in college, things changed. There was a marked transition. I started to feel I was ready for something more, and the timing just seemed right for things to happen differently.

What were some of your goals when you started college?
I knew that I wanted to study biology and genetics.

What do you do when you're not studying or going to classes?
Some of my recreational time is spent on languages or reading. I also

have a job at 3M. I like doing recombinant DNA research; I don't think I'd enjoy a job that involved working with literature or languages.

What are your goals for the future?
To get my Ph.D. and have a lab of my own.

Have you been labeled "gifted"? How do you feel about the label?
Yes, though I don't like the label. . . . I feel comfortable with the label if I'm in a group of people who are considered gifted — then I want to be considered gifted, too. But I'd certainly never introduce myself as a "gifted person." I'd never seek out that label, but I'd always want people to say, "Yeah, she's a bright student, she's an inquisitive student, she's going to go far." I think the label has positive and negative connotations.

What do you think "gifted" means?
I've met lots of people who get good grades and aren't interested in the learning process. They're much more interested in grades. To me, they are not gifted. They may be good test-takers or whatever, but they're not gifted. Gifted people question, and they love learning. They'll see a book and pick it up and love reading it, or they'll decide they want to learn to play the guitar and go out and do it. I guess I'm describing myself and the friends I have who I think are gifted. I'm constantly finding out that they're learning new things, making connections.

Who has the highest expectations of you?
First of all, myself, although I also have a tendency to let things slide. Then my mother shakes me by saying, "Hey, whatever happened to those expectations?" She helps me to come back and see what's within me.

How do you define success? How do you decide when you've done enough?
I'm not a perfectionist, which could be one of my downfalls. Sometimes, I get tired of something, and I'll finish it just to get it done. It may be less of a job than I originally intended.

What I think of as "good enough" changes from day to day, sometimes even hour to hour. I try as hard as I can to make every step of the way as enjoyable as possible. Then, no matter where I stop, I will have accomplished something. A lot of people put off that sense of accomplishment until the very end.

I look for ways to make things fun — or I look for ways to finish the project as quickly as possible.

Has there been one teacher, parent, or mentor who's been particularly helpful to you?
Undoubtedly, my mother. She's an incredible person. If I could choose to be like one person in the world, I'd choose my mother. She's the one person I'll always listen to. Sometimes, it's hard to have that one special person in the family, because you go through the normal rebellious stages of "No, I don't want to listen to you, I want to experience this myself."

My mother has guided me. She also knows when to let go. I don't think many parents know when to let go once they've had their say. I have a real stubborn streak, but my mother knows how to handle me when I get like that.

Would you describe yourself as a risk-taker?
Yes, maybe I take too many risks, because sometimes I get burned. But I always bounce back.

What do you like best about yourself? What's your greatest asset?
I think I have an easygoing personality — people feel comfortable around me. I like that about myself.

Are most of your friends gifted?
Yes. Some are risk-takers, too. Sometimes I try to start fires under the ones who don't take risks. People who don't risk are afraid of failure. Everyone has moments when they just don't feel good about themselves. Sometimes, I go and sulk for two or three hours, and then I get my "self" back. I think that people who have a low self-image have trouble taking risks because if they fail in one phase of their lives, they feel like they've failed in general.

I have friends from all over the world. Macalester is 10 percent international students. They're fun-loving people, kind people.

What's your greatest worry or biggest problem?
Every once in a while, I worry about living up to the expectations of

a few people who are important to me. I sometimes get anxiety attacks about it — I worry that I won't be what they thought I was or am. I'm not one to pretend I know things that I don't. I just hope they didn't make a mistake in thinking I can do all these great things!

What's your greatest nonacademic achievement?
I feel very lucky because I've worked to have a circle of friends I'm really close to. I make a strong effort to make friends. Sometimes, they just fall into my lap, but I do make an effort to meet new people when I get into a new situation.

What's your greatest academic achievement?
I guess I like where I am right now, majoring in biology. . . .I like how people perceive me as knowing a lot and having a lot of potential in this field.

Have you had any major disappointments in your life?
I never really had to study in high school. I was one of those students who got straight A's and never had to work at it. I never had to study if I didn't feel like doing it.

But then I started college and hit a wall. The studying was very different. The study habits I needed were different, and I didn't jump into it easily. It was hard making the transfer from high school to college, especially with grades.

What's your favorite goofing-off activity?
I live in a French language house right now. I like it when we all get kind of crazy and just dance around the house singing. It's totally spontaneous — you can't predict when it's going to happen. But it's fun.

Do you have a favorite daydream or fantasy?
I want to backpack around Europe for about two years and meet new people and see things.

Do you have an idol — someone you especially admire?
I like parts of a lot of different people. My mother is the only one I'd want to be like.

Are there any national or global issues that are of particular interest or concern to you?

It was hard for me when Reagan got reelected. At the time, that was a major concern. But right now, no.

If you could change one thing about the world, what would it be?

It's idealistic, but if people would just think more about others — how what they do affects others — the world would be better off. I wish I could cut out hypocrisy in the world — people who say one thing, then turn around and do the opposite.

Do you have any advice for other gifted teenagers?

I don't really feel I came into my own until college. High school was fun, but it's nowhere near what college is. If you have any problems now, just hang on, because college is going to be a blast! College is great. . . . I just love it.

INDEX

ABOUT THE AUTHORS

Jim Delisle is the author of *Gifted Children Speak Out* and numerous articles about gifted and talented youth. He has a Ph.D. in educational psychology and an M.Ed. in emotional disturbances and is currently an assistant professor of gifted education at Kent State University in Kent, Ohio. He has been a teacher of handicapped and gifted students.

Jim lives in Kent, Ohio with his wife, son, and four cats. His future goals include walking the Milford Track in New Zealand and visiting Antarctica and other out-of-the-way places.

Judy Galbraith is the author of *The Gifted Kids Survival Guides*. She is co-author with Connie Schmitz of *Managing the Social and Emotional Needs of the Gifted — A Teacher's Survival Guide*. She has a master's degree in guidance and counseling of the gifted and has worked with and taught gifted youth, their parents, and their teachers for over 10 years. In 1983, she started Free Spirit Publishing, which publishes books for gifted, talented, and creative kids.

Judy lives in Minneapolis, Minnesota with her dog, Woofie. Her future goals include taking a whole year off to do whatever she wants.